AI Engineering Starter Kit

The Practical Guide to Build, Train, and Deploy Real AI Applications with LLMs, MLOps, and Cutting-Edge Tools – Step-by-Step Projects for Aspiring AI Engineers

Nathan J. Halridge

Lucid Page Media
(an imprint of Orbita Media GmbH)
Ericusspitze 4
20457 Hamburg
Germany

Website: https://lucidpagemedia.com
Contact: contact@lucidpagemedia.com

1st Edition

ISBN: 978-3-69104-699-1

Table of contents

Introduction

Imagine stepping into a world where industries adapt at the speed of thought, where companies reach customers before problems even arise, and where new career paths open seemingly overnight. This isn't tomorrow's hope—it's today's reality for those harnessing the transformative power of AI engineering.

You've already seen pieces of this revolution: AI-driven chatbots resolving customer issues in seconds, personalized recommendations shaping your shopping experiences, and smart factories where predictive maintenance prevents costly equipment failures before they happen.

These aren't abstract concepts reserved for tech giants or research labs—they're the kinds of innovations skilled AI engineers are building every day. And you're just steps away from joining their ranks.

AI is Already Here: From Health to Retail to Manufacturing

HEALTH RETAIL MANUFACTURING

Yet, if you're holding this book, chances are you've also encountered some persistent myths about AI. Maybe you've thought, *"I'm not brilliant enough to break in,"* or *"My math skills aren't PhD-level,"* or even *"AI is too massive, mysterious, and complex for me to thrive in."* These beliefs keep talented, motivated people on the sidelines—watching as others build the future.

But here's the truth: real-world AI engineering is accessible, practical, and—most importantly—learnable by driven software developers and technology enthusiasts like you. This book is your invitation to set aside the intimidation and embrace hands-on learning with tools and techniques that demystify the field and turn curiosity into capability.

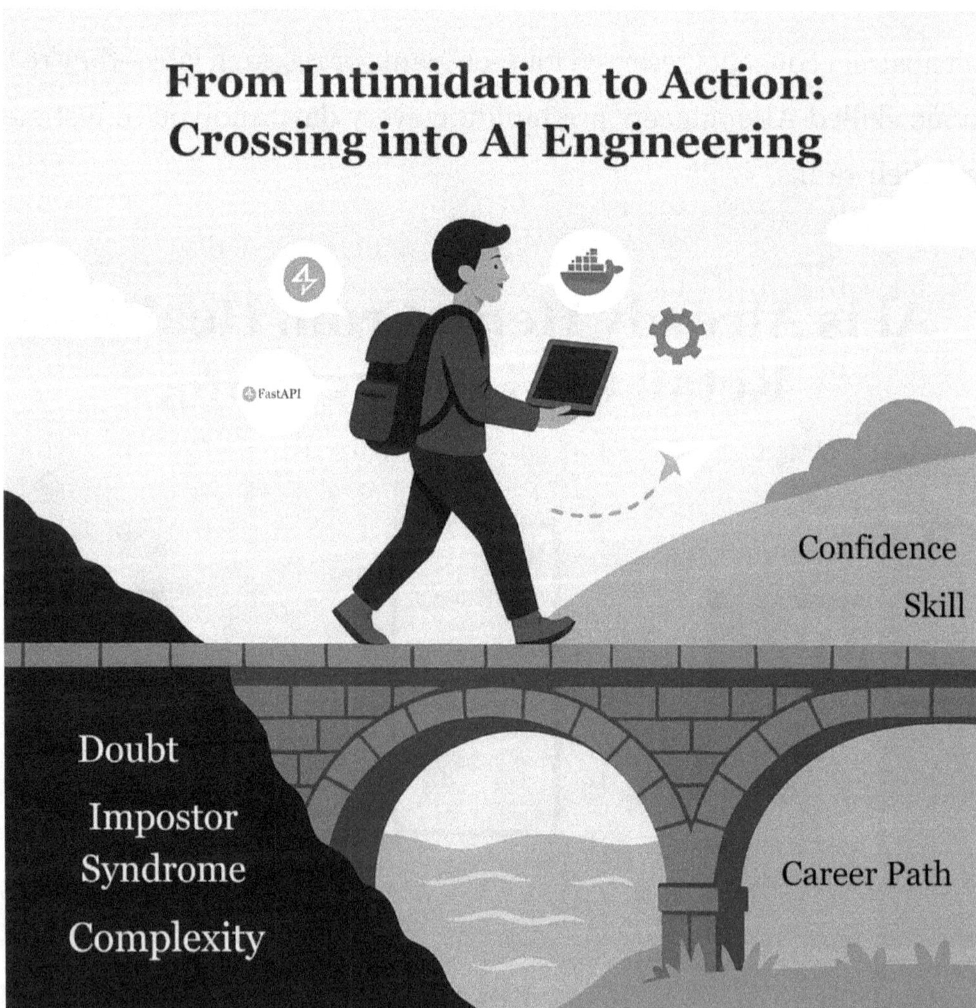

Let's clarify what AI engineering *really* means so you know exactly what you're signing up for. Unlike academic research or pure programming, AI engineering sits at the intersection of innovation and utility. It's the builder's realm—where models become products, algorithms evolve into deployed systems, and code translates directly into business value.

As an AI engineer, you don't just train models for the sake of experimentation—you architect, implement, and ship solutions that solve real problems. Whether it's deploying a recommendation engine to millions of users, packaging a model with Docker for smooth deployment, or monitoring system performance with MLflow, your job is to make AI tangible and impactful. That's what sets you apart from theorists or hobbyists. That's why AI engineering is one of the most in-demand skillsets in today's tech landscape.

This book isn't another theoretical overview or dense technical manual destined to collect dust on your shelf. The journey ahead is all about *doing*, not just reading. Every chapter includes practical, project-based exercises designed to help you evolve from a concept learner into a builder who sees real results.

By tackling real-world projects, deploying working AI applications, and integrating essential tools like FastAPI, Docker, and MLflow, you'll develop more than knowledge—you'll build a portfolio of functional, deployable systems. This portfolio will serve as a powerful testament to your skills, helping you stand out in the job market. Each exercise is carefully chosen for its relevance to how AI is built and deployed in modern organizations, ensuring you don't just follow instructions—you create real, showable solutions.

To smooth your path and accelerate your progress, this book includes a set of powerful companion resources. Early on, you'll gain access to our GitHub Portfolio Blueprint—a clear, professional guide to compiling, presenting, and explaining your projects. You'll also unlock the AI Career Kit, packed with resume boosters, customizable cover letter templates, and curated checklists to help you stand out in competitive job searches. These are the same strategies top engineers use to land interviews and demonstrate value.

The goal is simple: give you a complete toolkit that supports your learning, sharpens your message, and moves you quickly from skill-building to job applications—with confidence and clear evidence of what you can do.

The structure of this book follows a clear, logical roadmap. We'll begin with foundational concepts, ensuring everyone has the core understanding needed to define problems and choose effective solutions. From there, we'll move into the essential tools—Python libraries, frameworks, and ecosystem utilities every competent AI engineer uses.

Then, you'll progress through a series of hands-on tutorials that grow in complexity and realism: data ingestion, preprocessing, model training, evaluation, and fine-tuning. Next, we'll dive into deployment strategies, from containerization with Docker to API integration using FastAPI.

But no engineering system is complete without operational excellence—so you'll also learn industry practices for monitoring, logging, and iterative improvement, the kind of professional habits that distinguish AI engineers in the field. Finally, we'll focus on turning your skills into career traction: networking, technical interviews, and using your portfolio to reach the teams and roles that excite you most.

Each section builds on the last, guiding you step by step into deeper understanding—while reinforcing practical, job-ready skills at every turn.

Your AI Engineering Journey, Step by Step

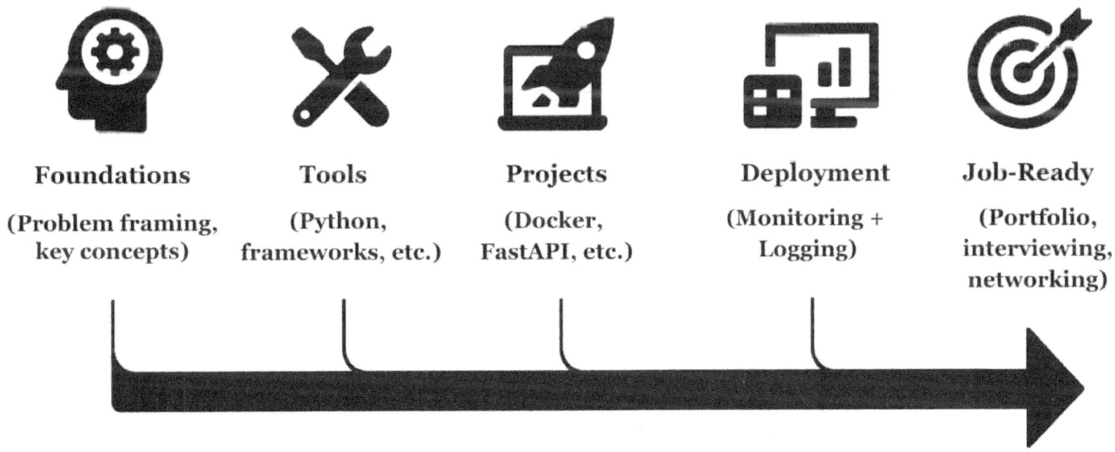

I understand that you may be balancing more than just this ambition. Many readers of this book are juggling demanding jobs, family obligations, or busy academic schedules. That's why the learning approach here is intentionally incremental and flexible. The exercises are modular—you can work through them one at a time, fit learning into your commutes or evenings, and revisit more challenging sections whenever you need reinforcement.

If you prefer to learn with others, group study suggestions and collaboration checklists are included to make teamwork seamless. Consistent, small efforts compound into meaningful progress. This book respects your time and your circumstances, helping you steadily build momentum—whether you have hours or just minutes to spare each day.

You have every reason to trust that this roadmap works. My own career has been shaped by years of building and deploying AI-powered solutions across industries—from finance and manufacturing to healthcare and e-commerce. I've worked with world-class teams, hired and mentored new engineers, and seen firsthand what separates those who dream from those who deliver.

Alongside my professional experience, the best research and industry practices have been distilled into approachable, actionable frameworks throughout this book. Every page reflects a commitment to clarity, accessibility, and real-world usefulness—a synthesis shaped on the frontlines of AI engineering.

If you've ever wondered whether now is the right time to act, let this be your signal: there's no better moment than today. The barriers to entry have never been lower, and the demand for builders—engineers who can design, ship, and maintain AI solutions—has never been higher.

By opening this book, you've already taken the first, most important step toward a future filled with possibilities you can shape. Your next breakthrough could redefine your career, your community, or even your own sense of what's possible.

So, why wait? Turn to Chapter 1, roll up your sleeves, and start building—just like thousands of others transforming their careers through AI engineering. Your future colleagues, your next employer, and your creative ambitions are waiting on the other side.

With the right guidance, supportive resources, and a focus on action over abstraction, the world of practical, impactful AI is yours to claim. Let's get started—your journey as an AI engineer begins now.

Chapter 1
AI Engineering Jumpstart: Unlocking the Future

Have you ever wondered what it takes to build intelligent systems that learn from data and make decisions like humans? How do AI engineers turn complex algorithms into practical tools used every day in fields like healthcare, finance, and manufacturing?

Many people assume that entering this field requires extraordinary talent or advanced math skills—but is that really true? What if hands-on experience and consistent practice mattered more than theoretical knowledge alone? These kinds of questions often discourage aspiring professionals from pursuing opportunities in AI engineering.

This chapter is here to challenge those assumptions and show how practical learning and real-world projects can open doors in this fast-growing career path. You'll discover how applying your skills step by step, using accessible tools, and building a strong portfolio can become the keys to success in AI engineering.

The Real-World Promise of AI Engineering

Artificial intelligence (AI) engineering sits at the crossroads of computer science, data analytics, and engineering—offering career paths that are rapidly outpacing traditional information technology (IT) roles. AI engineers design and refine algorithms that enable machines to mimic human reasoning, adapt to new data, and make complex decisions.

Unlike conventional IT professionals—who typically manage existing systems, networks, or code within predefined frameworks—AI engineers focus on innovation. They build intelligent, adaptive solutions from scratch or enhance existing systems for smarter performance. For instance, while an IT systems administrator might troubleshoot server issues, an AI engineer develops models that predict and prevent server failures before they occur (Johns Hopkins University, 2024).

Key technical skills for this transition include deep learning, neural networks, big data processing, and natural language processing (NLP). These capabilities allow engineers to deliver unique, future-facing solutions. One emerging example is the role of the prompt engineer—someone who crafts inputs that guide AI systems toward balanced,

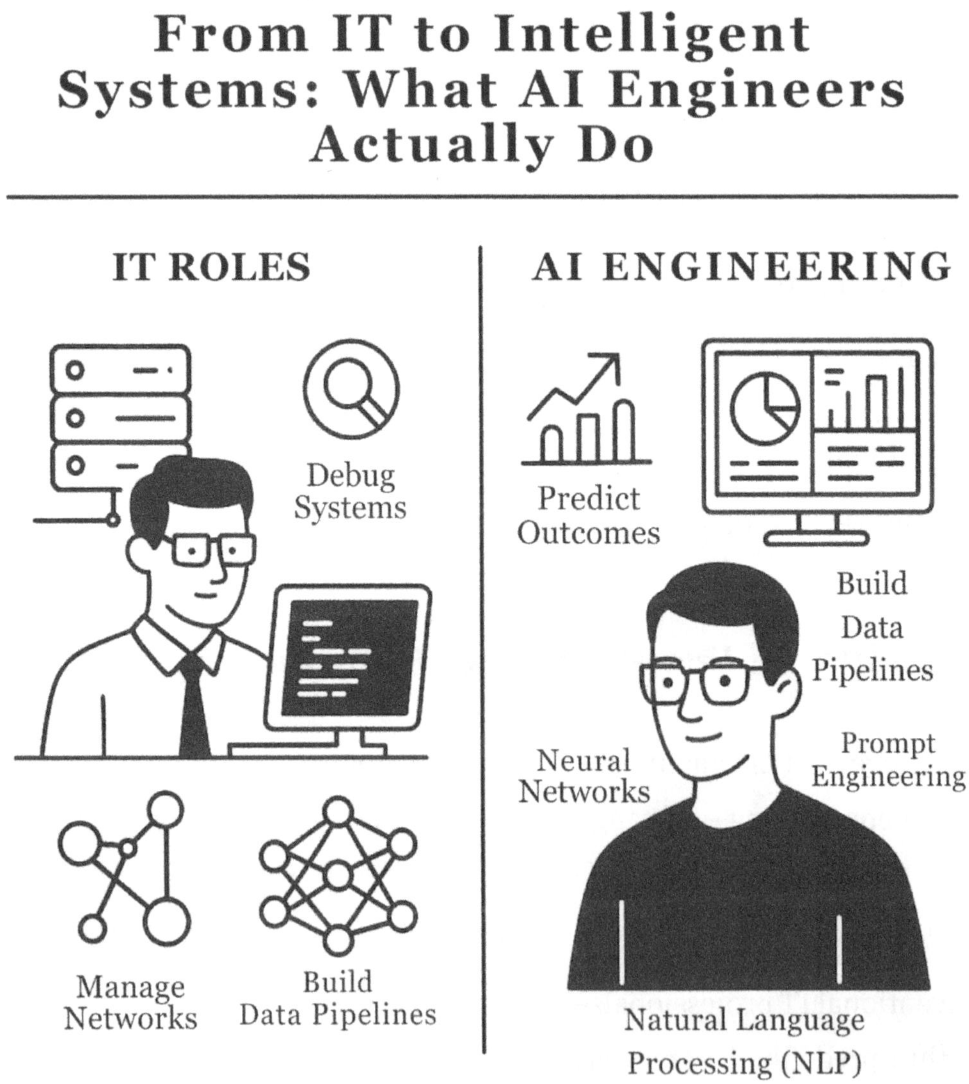

accurate results—a job that didn't even exist a decade ago (University of San Diego, 2024).

In terms of real job titles, the market demands AI specialists across a wide range of roles: machine learning engineer, NLP specialist, AI ethicist, AI prompt engineer, and robotics automation engineer (University of San Diego, 2024). These professionals work in sectors well beyond traditional tech companies, including automotive, aerospace, healthcare, and finance.

Salary and employment trends confirm this shift: median salaries for machine learning engineers in the U.S. routinely exceed $120,000, with LinkedIn reporting a 74% annual growth in AI-related roles between 2016 and 2021. Major employers like Google, IBM, and Amazon regularly list thousands of openings for AI professionals—evidence of rapid and sustained career expansion.

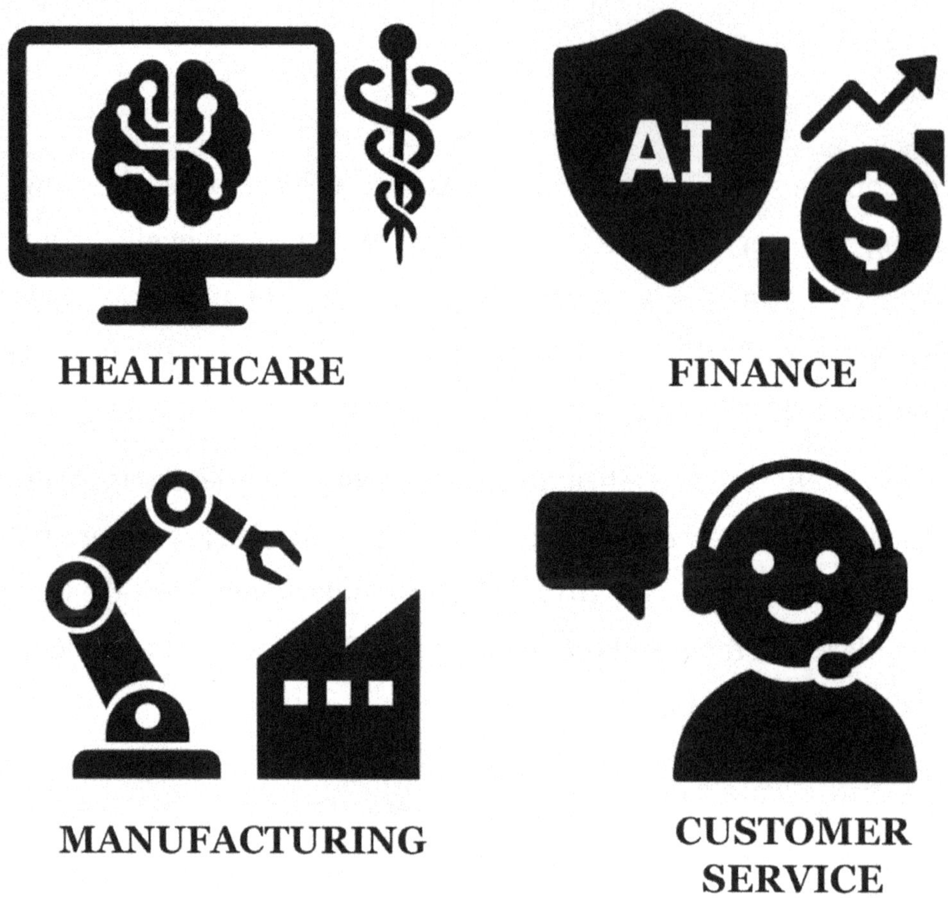

AI-driven innovation is now transforming industries that were once slow to evolve. In healthcare, AI is revolutionizing diagnostic precision and speed. At Memorial Sloan Kettering Cancer Center, advanced deep learning models analyze mammograms and pathology slides, achieving breast cancer detection rates of up to 99% while reducing diagnostic errors among radiologists. The University of California, San Francisco, uses AI-powered language processing to summarize patient histories and suggest treatment plans, harnessing vast volumes of medical data to improve outcomes and efficiency. These applications save time—and lives—with measurable results.

In finance, AI serves as a powerful tool against fraud and cyber threats. J.P. Morgan's COiN platform uses natural language processing and machine learning to process millions of legal documents, extracting key information in seconds rather than hours. Capital One's AI-powered fraud detection system prevented over $150 million in fraudulent transactions in a single year, using machine learning to scan millions of transactions for suspicious patterns—dramatically reducing false positives and improving customer protection.

In manufacturing, AI enables predictive maintenance and robotics automation. Siemens and General Electric deploy machine learning models on production lines to monitor sensor data—such as temperature, vibration, and equipment usage—to forecast and prevent failures before they happen (Johns Hopkins University, 2024). Ford Motor Company, for instance, reduced assembly line downtime by 30% after implementing AI-driven predictive maintenance, saving millions annually. Meanwhile, companies like Fanuc use neural networks for real-time quality control, cutting defective output by up to 70%.

AI's problem-solving capabilities also deliver direct efficiency gains in customer service and logistics. Bank of America's Erica chatbot handles over 10 million customer interactions per month, reducing average wait times by 65% and deflecting up to 30% of routine inquiries from human agents to intelligent automation. In logistics, Amazon leverages AI to optimize supply chains—balancing demand forecasts, warehouse locations, and delivery routes—which has cut delivery times by 40% while slashing operational costs (Johns Hopkins University, 2024).

Startups are fueling much of this sector's momentum. Scale AI, which provides data labeling services for autonomous vehicles, recently reached a $7 billion valuation. Olive, a health-tech startup, uses AI to automate insurance claims processing, freeing hospital staff from repetitive administrative work. UiPath, a leader in robotic process automation

(RPA), is valued at over $10 billion and continues expanding globally to meet surging demand for AI-powered business automation tools.

Hiring trends reflect a global appetite for AI engineers. According to the World Economic Forum's *Future of Jobs* report, demand for AI and big data skills is expected to grow by 16% through 2025 (University of San Diego, 2024). While major tech hubs like San Francisco, Toronto, London, and Bangalore lead in recruitment, sectors such as healthcare, automotive, and finance are also aggressively competing for AI talent.

This clear, data-backed evolution underscores the urgent need for professionals who can build, refine, and govern the next wave of AI-driven solutions. It challenges the perception that the field is inaccessible—and lays the groundwork for a deeper exploration of the myths and realities shaping AI engineering today.

Breaking the Myths: AI Engineering Demystified

Many people assume that only rare geniuses can succeed in AI engineering. This "genius myth" discourages capable individuals from even attempting to enter the field. In reality, AI engineering is a skill developed through repeated effort, feedback, and everyday problem-solving. Some of today's most accomplished AI engineers began with modest coding abilities, often acquired through short courses, after-school programs, or online tutorials. Through steady engagement and persistence, they built their competence step by step.

A widely cited example involves self-taught programmers who started with basic Python scripts and eventually contributed to open-source AI projects—progressing to roles at top technology companies. This incremental, experience-driven approach reflects a larger truth: in technology, consistent practice often matters more than innate brilliance (Hornberger et al., 2023). For readers, the takeaway is clear—patience, curiosity, and hands-on repetition are more valuable than any supposed natural gift.

Another common misconception is that strong math skills—particularly in calculus—are essential for all AI engineering roles. While theoretical researchers may rely heavily on advanced linear algebra, calculus, and statistics, most practical engineering roles require only a foundational understanding of key concepts. Entry-level AI engineers benefit from knowing basic algebra, probability, and statistics, which are useful for interpreting model outputs and evaluating performance.

Thanks to modern libraries and frameworks, much of the underlying complexity is abstracted away. Tools like TensorFlow, Keras, and Scikit-Learn let you apply powerful machine learning algorithms with only a conceptual grasp of how they work "under the hood" (Why Age 13–19 Is Ideal for Learning AI: The Science behind Teen AI Mastery – LearnWithPride, 2025). Rather than deriving gradients or probability functions by hand, engineers focus on building pipelines, tuning models, and interpreting results. In this way, math becomes a helpful tool—accessible when needed, but not a rigid barrier.

Employers, too, are shifting focus from theory to practice. When hiring AI engineers, they increasingly prioritize hands-on experience: working with real datasets, contributing to collaborative projects, participating in hackathons, or solving practical coding challenges. They want to see that candidates have deployed models, used Git for version control, or collaborated in team-based environments.

Job descriptions frequently list requirements such as "Experience with Python and TensorFlow," "Ability to handle large datasets," or "Strong debugging skills," while omitting expectations around advanced math unless the role is research-focused. Employers are also showing growing interest in prompt engineering and AI interaction design—skills often developed through experimentation and real-world use, not academic study (Why Age 13–19 Is Ideal for Learning AI: The Science behind Teen AI Mastery – LearnWithPride, 2025). Research confirms that learners who gain hands-on exposure and apply their skills in projects are better prepared for the workplace (Hornberger et al., 2023)

The technical barriers to AI engineering have dropped dramatically thanks to accessible platforms and open-source libraries. In the past, building an AI model required deep programming knowledge and expensive hardware. Today, platforms like Google Colab offer free, cloud-based environments where learners can run Python code instantly. Libraries such as NumPy and Pandas simplify data handling, while TensorFlow, Keras, and Scikit-Learn provide plug-and-play models for machine learning.

Even beginners with basic programming skills can build functioning models from day one. Tools like Visual Studio Code and Jupyter Notebook make coding more readable and interactive, further lowering the learning curve (Why Age 13–19 Is Ideal for Learning AI: The Science behind Teen AI Mastery – LearnWithPride, 2025). Recent studies even show teenagers using these tools to complete sophisticated projects—from building chatbots for classmates to analyzing real-world issues with machine learning.

Practical Pathways into AI Engineering

The most reliable way into the field is to begin with small programming projects and gradually explore AI libraries. Many successful learners gain momentum by solving real problems—automating tasks, analyzing personal data, or joining online competitions—rather than waiting for perfect theoretical preparation.

Finding mentors and participating in learning communities, whether online or through school, provides valuable feedback and direction. Building a portfolio of practical, relevant projects helps learners showcase their skills in ways that employers respect.

This approach offers a clear, empowering entry point into AI engineering. You don't need genius, advanced math, or expensive tools—just curiosity, consistency, and a willingness to engage with real problems (Hornberger et al., 2023; Why Age 13–19 Is Ideal for Learning AI: The Science behind Teen AI Mastery – LearnWithPride, 2025).

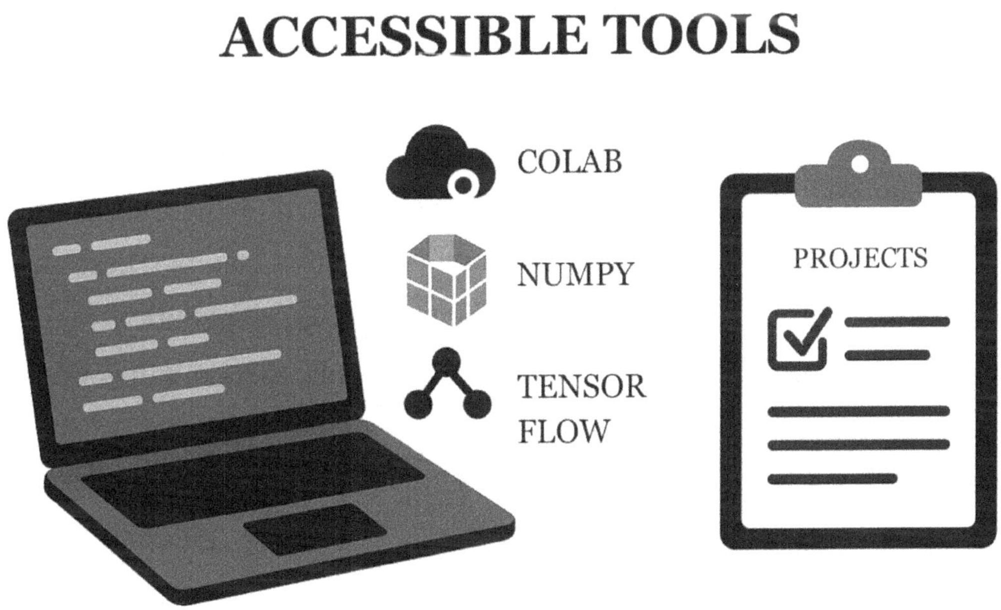

Project First, Theory Second: Winning by Doing

Knowledge Retention Through Application

Engaging directly with hands-on projects cements knowledge in ways that lectures and theory alone cannot. When learners build something tangible, every line of code and design decision becomes an active memory anchor. For example, creating an AI model to classify handwritten digits with a neural network teaches far more about machine learning than simply reading about it.

Project work reveals subtleties—like data preprocessing, hyperparameter tuning, and debugging logic errors—that theory keeps abstract. These challenges—and the process of overcoming them—deepen understanding and promote long-term retention (Northwest, n.d.). Facing real implementation roadblocks forces learners to revisit and reinforce the underlying theory, transforming short-term recall into durable knowledge.

Hands-on work also highlights the difference between knowing *what* and knowing *how*. A student might recite the steps of gradient descent, but implementing it reveals why some algorithms converge faster or how learning rates affect results. These experiences expose hidden knowledge gaps and strengthen fluency, adaptability, and technical resilience (Schools, 2025). Abstract concepts become tools learners can confidently use.

Portfolio Development Impact

In AI and tech roles, employers care less about transcripts and more about real-world evidence. A portfolio of completed, relevant projects demonstrates initiative, technical skill, and problem-solving ability.
For example, a candidate applying for a data science role might include a movie recommendation engine or a visualization of large-scale social trends. Strong portfolios feature concise write-ups outlining the problem, tech stack, challenges faced, and measurable outcomes—like performance improvements or user feedback. Repositories, demo videos, and interactive dashboards offer concrete proof of capability.

Portfolios often outweigh academic credentials. Given two applicants—one with straight As in AI coursework and another with a slightly lower GPA but multiple public projects on GitHub—the latter typically stands out. They've demonstrated applied knowledge (Schools, 2025).

Modern portfolios also include annotated code, explanatory blog posts, and user testimonials, giving hiring managers insight into a candidate's creativity, communication skills, and growth trajectory—traits grades alone can't capture (Northwest, n.d.).

Interview Performance

Hands-on experience turns interviews into storytelling opportunities. Candidates can reference specific projects, describing how they debugged a failing model, adopted a new framework under pressure, or optimized a chatbot in production (Schools, 2025).

This approach showcases real problem-solving and strategic thinking. Interviewers are impressed by candidates who can walk through system architecture, discuss design trade-offs, and explain performance or security decisions.

In live coding segments, experience with different APIs or frameworks builds confidence. By referencing portfolio projects, candidates highlight not only their technical range but also soft skills like collaboration and initiative. Sharing code samples, demo links, or live apps makes responses memorable and credible (Northwest, n.d.).

Technical Skill Integration

AI projects require interdisciplinary skills—not just writing models but also managing data, designing interfaces, applying security basics, and handling feedback. A single project might involve Python scripting, SQL databases, TensorFlow for training, and React for user interaction. These skills mirror real production environments.

Projects also teach version control, testing, deployment, and monitoring—skills often underemphasized in academia. Learners gain familiarity with tools like Git, Docker, and cloud platforms. In team projects, they also learn documentation, task management, and peer reviews—habits that employers highly value (Schools, 2025).

Taking a project from concept to deployment means navigating real-world ambiguity and iteration—skills essential in fast-paced tech careers (Northwest, n.d.).

Real Projects = Real Skills in Action

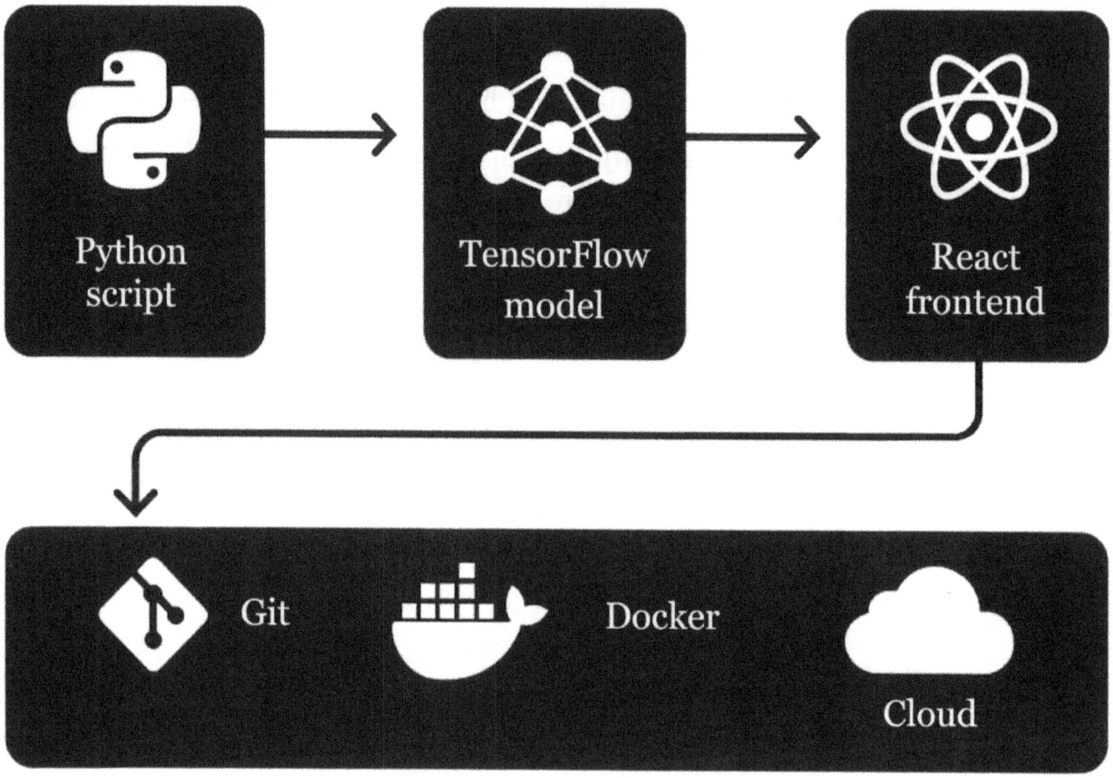

Bonuses That Deliver: Tools for Real Success

At the heart of a strong AI application is a clear, professional portfolio. The **Portfolio Blueprint** helps organize your GitHub repositories: code, data, documentation, and results go in clearly named folders. Each project includes a standardized README with sections like overview, installation, usage, highlights, and insights.

This structure allows recruiters to quickly assess your work. A well-documented machine learning project might feature a performance table, links to Jupyter notebooks, and bullet-point takeaways—all visible at a glance. Clean, consistent documentation makes even a simple regression model appear career-ready (luminousmen, 2022).

Strong candidates also write READMEs that explain not just what was built, but how, why, and what they'd improve next—revealing mindset and growth potential.

Resume Accelerators provide pre-written, results-focused bullet points tailored for AI and software roles. For example:
✓ "Improved model inference speed by 30% using TensorRT optimization"

✗ "Worked on making models faster".

Good entries include metrics or scope:
✓ "Deployed chatbot solution supporting 50,000 users via AWS Lambda"
These outperform vague statements and pass applicant tracking systems (ATS) with relevant keywords (Job, 2025).

Checklists of strong vs. weak bullet points make improvement easy:
✓ "Automated data cleaning with pandas, cutting preprocessing time by 90%"

✗ "Worked with data using Python"
With the Accelerators, you upgrade your resume line by line with confidence.

Career Kit Checklists break your job search into weekly actions:
– Refresh portfolio content
– Apply to 5 tailored roles
– Attend 1 AI event

– Update LinkedIn headline
– Publish a blog post or project update

Before interviews, you're prompted to rehearse STAR-format responses and prepare stories showcasing both technical and interpersonal wins. Networking goals include reaching out to new contacts, joining open-source events, and sharing your work on forums. These systems promote consistent, visible engagement (luminousmen, 2022).

Showcase Power tips help you stand out:
– Pin top GitHub repos
– Use tags like "NLP" or "FastAPI" in project descriptions
– Add README badges for tests or build status
– Embed demo videos or GIFs

On LinkedIn, your summary highlights key skills and results. Your activity reflects contributions to open-source, comments on AI posts, or sharing your learning milestones—actions that boost discoverability. AI communities on Slack, Discord, and X provide additional visibility and learning opportunities (Job, 2025).

How to Use This Book to Transform Your Career

Busy professionals thrive with incremental learning. Break complex topics into short, consistent sessions—20 to 30 minutes per day works better than weekend marathons (Jankowski, 2018).

Use digital calendars to block learning slots. Store materials in the cloud for quick access during breaks or commutes. Set micro-goals: read two pages, review a concept, or write a basic function. Divide complex chapters into 3–5 daily objectives—for example, learn convolution one day, activation functions the next.

Solo learners can use techniques like:
- Coding small examples
- Practicing flashcards
- Speaking or sketching concepts from memory
- Using spaced-repetition apps

These approaches reinforce memory while keeping effort manageable (Stine-Morrow et al., 2014).

Group learning offers structure and feedback. Small teams can meet weekly for peer reviews, project updates, or code walkthroughs. Round-robin teaching and collaborative coding keep sessions engaging and productive.

Hybrid learning works too: study solo, then share questions or insights with a group asynchronously or via short calls.

Track progress with simple metrics:
– Chapters completed
– Projects launched
– Code problems solved

Use a weekly self-review: what did you learn, where are the gaps, and what's next?

Peer feedback deepens reflection. Swap code or write-ups, use scoring rubrics, and rotate who leads the session. Structure brings accountability and builds a stronger learning loop.

Finally, apply AI at work. Automate reports, analyze internal data, or optimize a small workflow. Document impact—time saved, errors reduced, outcomes improved. These small wins showcase applied value and build credibility.

Track business metrics tied to your work—cost savings, improved insights, or efficiency boosts—and collect feedback from managers. These accomplishments can drive promotions, portfolio visibility, and future opportunities (Stine-Morrow et al., 2014; Jankowski, 2018).

Tiny Routines, Big Impact

Final Thoughts

Now that we've explored the transformative impact of AI engineering, dispelled common misconceptions, and highlighted the value of hands-on learning supported by practical tools, you're ready to engage with this dynamic field with confidence.

By applying the strategies and resources outlined in this chapter, you'll develop real-world skills, build a compelling portfolio, and navigate your career path with clarity and purpose. Whether you're starting from scratch or transitioning from a software development background, adopting a project-based approach will deepen your understanding and equip you for the evolving demands of AI roles across industries.

With consistent effort and the right support, you're fully prepared to take the next step—and unlock the full potential of AI engineering in your professional journey.

Chapter 2

AI Engineering Unpacked: The Essentials and the Pitfalls

The demand for AI engineers has more than doubled in just a few years, with over 180,000 job openings in the United States alone as of 2023. Yet despite this explosive growth, many newcomers quickly realize that knowing algorithms and theory is not enough.

True success in AI engineering comes from mastering a hands-on craft—one that transforms abstract models into robust, scalable systems used by millions. This chapter challenges conventional assumptions about what it really means to be an AI engineer and explains why practical skills, a problem-solving mindset, and full end-to-end ownership matter far more than academic knowledge alone.
Understanding these fundamentals isn't just helpful—it's essential for building a career that delivers real-world results in today's fast-evolving AI landscape.

Defining AI Engineering as a Hands-On Discipline

AI engineering is fundamentally a builder's science—focused on constructing real systems that function reliably in the world. Unlike pure research, which may conclude with mathematical proofs or simulation results, AI engineering demands the translation of solutions into production-ready software. Engineers take theoretical concepts and turn them into robust models, APIs, dashboards, or full applications that people can use.

For example, rather than just studying natural language processing, an AI engineer might build a sentiment analysis API that integrates into a client's customer service platform. This builder's mindset shows up in daily practices like continuous code deployment, version control, and rigorous code reviews—all essential to ensure new features work in real environments. In a practical setting, choosing to ship a functional recommendation engine on time, rather than endlessly tuning hyperparameters, means users benefit immediately from personalized experiences (Benigni, 2025).

This hands-on approach is inseparable from a strong emphasis on functional, maintainable code. AI engineers constantly create, test, and refine code bases for specific use cases—whether designing neural network services with TensorFlow, integrating ML pipelines with CI/CD tools, or automating model retraining with cloud functions.

Often, clean, reliable code is valued more than knowledge of cutting-edge algorithms. In practice, a batch job that maintains 99.9% uptime or a chatbot that handles support tickets without crashing holds far more value than a "state-of-the-art" prototype trapped in a slide deck. This focus on working solutions drives AI engineers to address real user needs, solve concrete business problems, and close the gap between research and application (Benigni, 2025).

AI engineering projects span the entire lifecycle—from initial ideation and data collection to model monitoring and ongoing iteration. The process begins with gathering requirements and defining the problem, followed by architectural design, data preparation, and model development. Engineers then validate models through testing, package them using tools like Docker, deploy via cloud services such as AWS or GCP, and set up monitoring for performance, drift, and reliability.

In many cases, a single engineer or small team owns the full journey—from data exploration in Python to deployment on Kubernetes—ensuring seamless integration of every component. And ownership doesn't end at launch: AI engineers are responsible for model retraining, handling production incidents, and scaling systems as demand grows. For example, building and deploying a fraud detection model for a bank involves cleaning transactional data, selecting the architecture, building feature stores, integrating with transaction systems, and designing dashboards for analyst review. This full-stack responsibility keeps engineers tightly aligned with both technical outcomes and business goals (Masood, 2025).

To thrive in this role, an AI engineer must master a hybrid skillset that blends software engineering, machine learning, cloud infrastructure, and domain-specific knowledge. Core languages like Python, Java, and Scala pair with deep familiarity with ML libraries such as PyTorch, TensorFlow, and scikit-learn. Infrastructure tools like Docker, Kubernetes, and AWS SageMaker support streamlined development and deployment. Strong database skills (SQL, NoSQL) and Git version control are essential.

Engineers must navigate across technical boundaries: from extracting and engineering features from sales data, to deploying scalable REST APIs, to automating pipelines with tools like Jenkins or GitHub Actions. In fintech, for instance, an engineer may combine deep learning, cloud security, and fraud detection to build a real-time transaction scoring engine. This integration of skills transforms isolated prototypes into business-critical systems (Masood, 2025).

Ultimately, **deliverables define success** in AI engineering. What matters most is what works in the real world—not what's theoretically elegant. Employers and stakeholders focus on tangible outcomes: improved conversion rates, reduced churn, fewer manual processes, faster system responses, or decreased false positives.

Key metrics like latency (e.g., milliseconds per prediction), uptime (e.g., 99.9% availability), accuracy (e.g., precision, recall, AUC), and business KPIs shape hiring, promotions, and funding. For example, when an AI assistant improves customer satisfaction and reduces support tickets, the engineer's contribution is measured by impact, not implementation complexity. Peer reviews, product launches, and stakeholder evaluations all return to one point: what value did this system deliver?

This results-driven culture forms a feedback loop that motivates engineers to focus on quantifiable improvements, always tying their efforts to real users, products, and outcomes (Benigni, 2025; Masood, 2025).

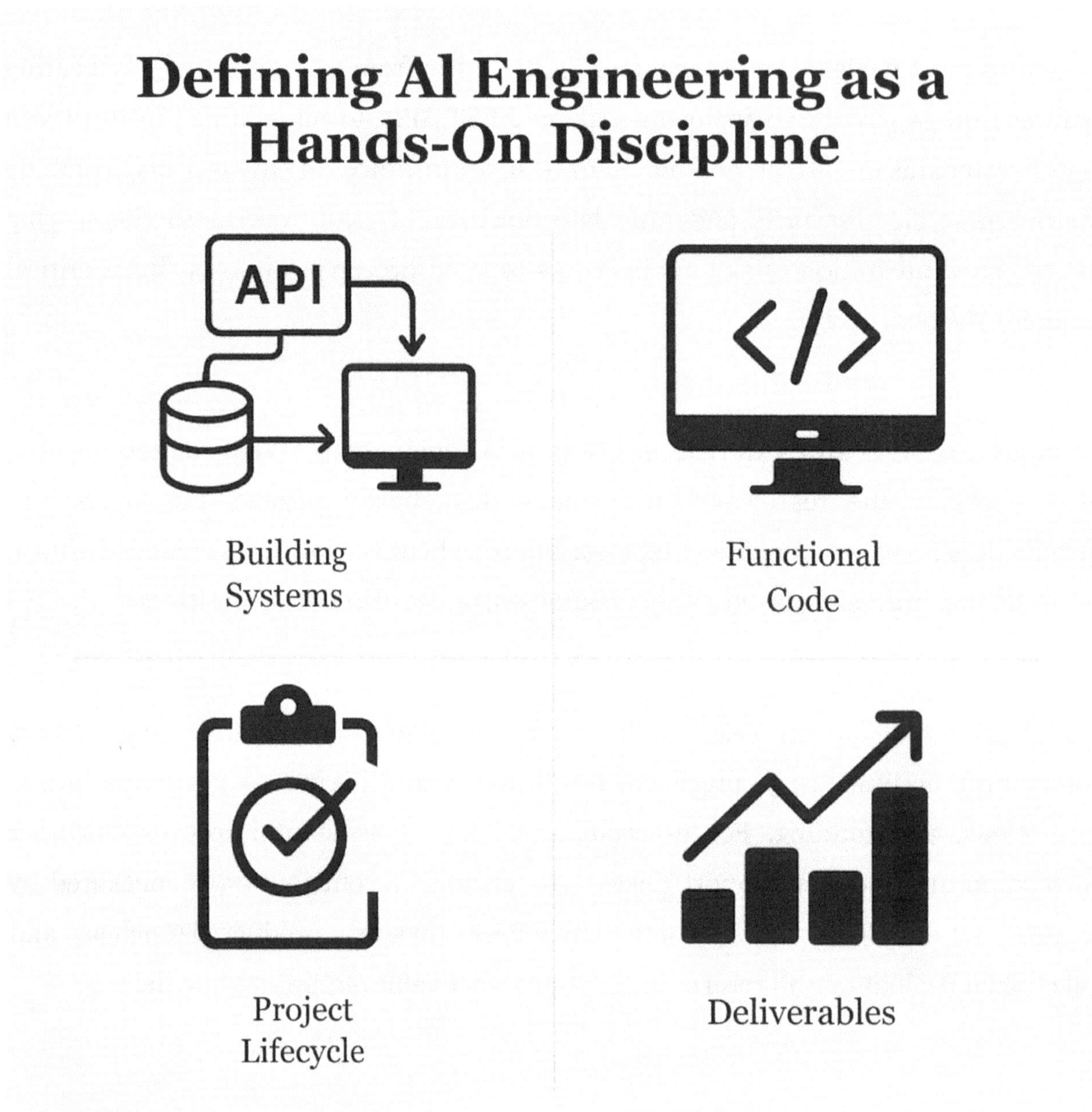

By combining a builder's mindset, end-to-end ownership, a cross-disciplinary skillset, and a relentless focus on results, AI engineering elevates the practical over the theoretical—delivering solutions that matter far beyond the lab.

Understanding the Difference: Theory-Only vs. Applied AI Engineering

Many entering the AI field bring strong theoretical backgrounds, only to find themselves at a crossroads when theory alone fails to produce real results. Take, for example, a job applicant with a PhD in machine learning who excels at deriving loss functions and analyzing model complexity. When placed in a production environment, that same candidate might struggle immediately.

Asked to integrate a sentiment analysis model into a web service, they may find containerization with Docker or deployment automation using cloud tools unfamiliar. Debugging inference issues—like latency spikes or out-of-memory errors at scale—often leaves theory-only experts searching for help. Collaboration can also be a hurdle: using Git for version control or resolving merge conflicts in a team setting may be entirely new territory. Employers quickly notice these gaps, especially when candidates are asked to walk through practical problem-solving scenarios, either on the job or during technical interviews (Aijobs.net Will Become Foo🦍 – Visit Foorilla.com!, 2024).

A solid theoretical foundation is valuable, but without a portfolio of real-world projects, candidates often go overlooked in competitive hiring pools. Employers want proof that applicants can handle messy, ambiguous problems—the kind that don't come with clean answers in a textbook. Portfolios featuring functional demos stand out.

Consider a candidate who builds a full customer review analysis pipeline: collecting data from APIs, preprocessing it in Jupyter notebooks, training models in PyTorch, and deploying a real-time dashboard using Flask and AWS Lambda. Or someone who develops a fraud detection microservice integrated with Stripe's API, delivering real-time predictions and sending alerts via Slack. These examples show not only technical depth, but the ability to deliver reliable, integrated systems under real constraints. Practical engineering is as much about "what works" as "what's possible"—and strong portfolios prove it (Chiu et al., 2024).

Deployment, in particular, is a space where theory rarely holds up on its own. A model that performs well in academic benchmarks might fail in production due to differences in data distribution, hardware limitations, or user load.

An AI scientist might build a highly accurate recommender system locally, only to find it unusable online due to slow response times. Cloud-based deployments can introduce cold start latency, forcing engineers to redesign how models initialize. API integration adds another layer of complexity: models must communicate with other microservices using REST or messaging systems, which involve serialization, error handling, and rate limits. Scaling further increases the challenge—managing GPU sharing, sharding across data centers, and deploying updates via blue-green strategies.

These are the pain points that affect real users, real products, and business success. Employers are looking for engineers who can anticipate and resolve them (Aijobs.net Will Become Foo🦍 – Visit Foorilla.com!, 2024).

AI engineering also doesn't happen in isolation. Daily work involves collaboration across roles and functions. Engineers must explain implementation choices during code reviews, respond to peer feedback on performance or security, and align efforts with broader team goals.

In sprint planning, AI engineers work alongside data scientists, backend developers, designers, and product managers. One day might involve coordinating GPU access for deep learning training; the next, negotiating CI/CD pipeline decisions with DevOps. Shifting business priorities are common, leading to mid-sprint pivots or realignment discussions. Often, finishing a task depends on another teammate completing theirs first—making communication, planning, and flexibility essential.

Those used to working in isolation may find these realities overwhelming. Success in AI engineering requires strong interpersonal skills: giving and receiving feedback, mentoring peers, and adapting to team dynamics (Chiu et al., 2024).

Ultimately, concrete, real-world skills are what drive product impact when stakes are high. A candidate who understands only the theory may freeze if their code causes 2% downtime in a live trading system. A practical engineer knows how to triage the issue, roll back safely, and restore service with minimal impact.

This is why employers prioritize engineers with deployment experience, team reliability, and a strong project record. These are the qualities that bring AI from research into production—and make it usable, scalable, and impactful (Aijobs.net Will Become Foo🦍 – Visit Foorilla.com!, 2024; Chiu et al., 2024).

The Urgency and Opportunity of AI Engineering Today

AI Engineering Job Growth and Market Dynamics

AI engineering roles are experiencing explosive demand across every major sector. In 2023, the United States alone listed over 180,000 job postings requiring machine learning skills—nearly double the number from just three years earlier. Tech hubs like San Francisco, New York, and London now post tens of thousands of openings focused on data science, AI research, and model deployment. Healthcare and finance lead the way, with nearly one in five new roles requesting AI development capabilities. Countries investing in energy transition and climate analytics are also reporting sharp increases in hiring for AI engineers—those who can build predictive models, optimize supply chains, or power green technologies (OECD, 2025).

Globally, AI adoption is accelerating across industries. In manufacturing, 42% of surveyed companies reported having at least one AI project in production by 2023—up from just 28% in 2021. Retail, logistics, and agriculture are close behind, leveraging AI to automate processes, predict demand, and personalize products.

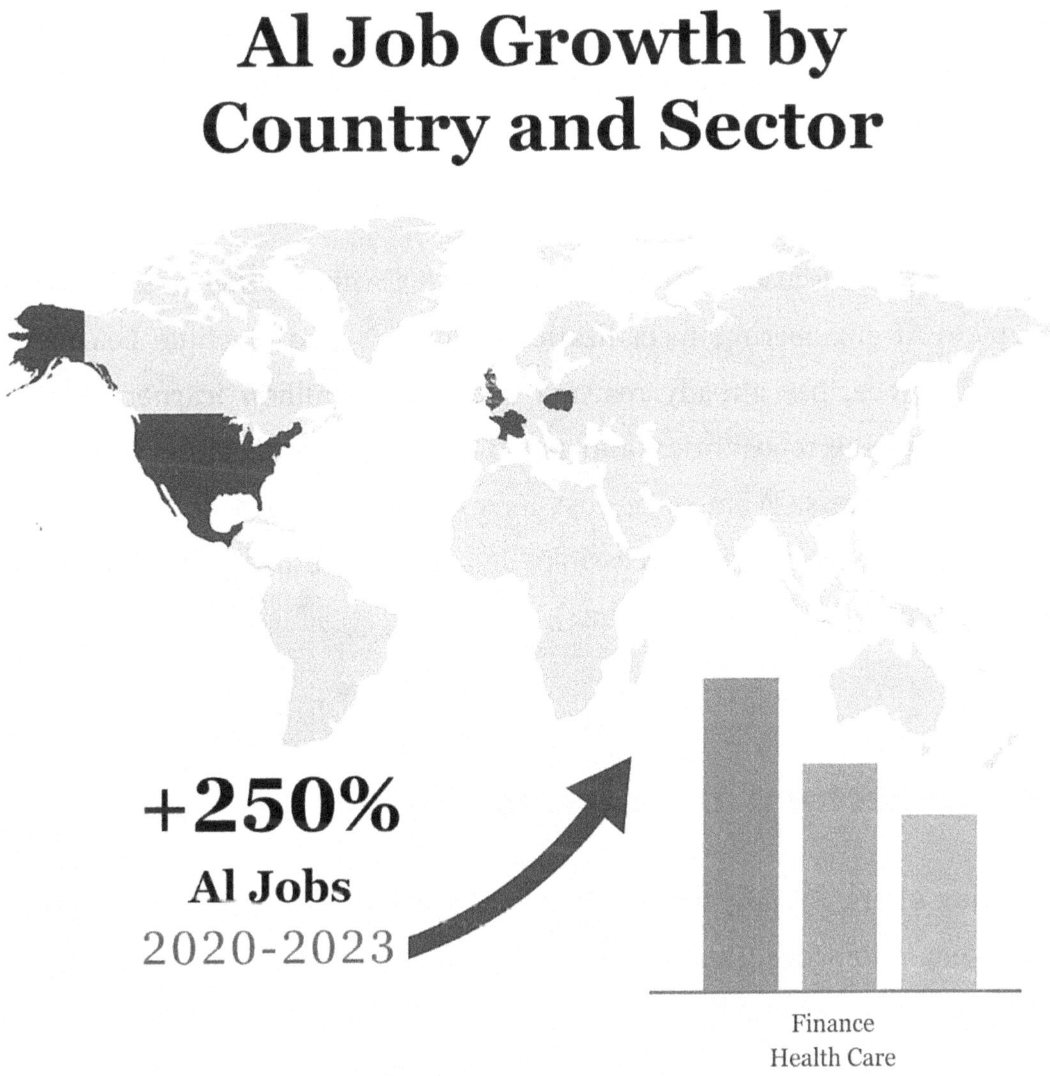

These trends are unmistakable: the landscape is shifting fast, and the growing number of roles signals a clear opportunity. For those with practical AI engineering skills, it's a seller's market (Sharps, 2024; OECD, 2025).

Accessible Tools and Platforms

The barriers to entry into AI engineering have fallen dramatically thanks to open-source tools and affordable cloud services. Frameworks like TensorFlow and PyTorch are entirely free and come with robust online documentation. Tools such as Jupyter Notebooks and Google Colab let users build and run machine learning models without expensive hardware. Even major cloud providers like AWS and Microsoft Azure now offer free-tier credits for students and new developers.

Learning resources have also expanded rapidly. MOOCs like Coursera, edX, and Udacity offer complete AI engineering specializations. Google's free Machine Learning Crash Course, for instance, has already reached over half a million learners. Community forums, public GitHub repositories, and group programming meetups reduce isolation and accelerate progress. What once cost tens of thousands of dollars and required university access is now globally accessible—letting anyone with a laptop and internet connection skill up at scale (Sharps, 2024).

Career Trajectory and Lasting Value

AI engineering offers not only immediate job access but also long-term career growth. In top markets, entry-level salaries exceed $110,000. With five years of deployment experience, that number often doubles—especially in fast-growing sectors like biotech, energy, and autonomous systems. Career changers have found remarkable success: a mechanical engineer in Detroit learns Python and TensorFlow online and, within 18 months, secures a lead AI role at an automotive startup building self-driving tech. An operations analyst in Singapore studies NLP for eight months and lands a remote AI consulting job, tripling their income and gaining global reach.

Even seasoned professionals use AI to pivot or accelerate their careers. Many early-career software developers, for example, report that earning AI certifications allowed them to move into lead or architect positions within two years, where they set technical direction and oversee teams. These skills also provide resilience: rather than risk being replaced by automation, AI engineers are the ones designing and improving the systems that drive automation itself (Sharps, 2024).

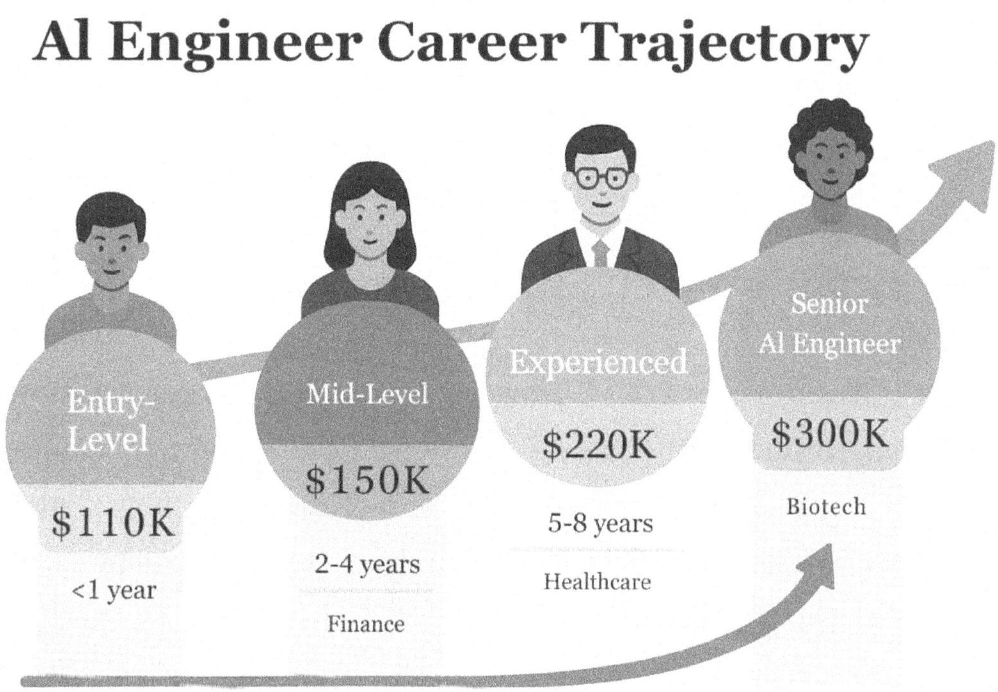

The Cost of Waiting: Industry Cases

Delaying AI skill development carries real risk. Some of the most dramatic examples come from legacy companies: numerous brick-and-mortar retailers lost market share to competitors that embraced AI-powered logistics, pricing, and customer analytics. Early adopters in logistics—like UPS—used predictive routing and real-time engine diagnostics well before others, saving costs and gaining reliability. Those who waited too long often faced shrinking margins, layoffs, or bankruptcy.

On an individual level, professionals have seen their roles transformed or phased out. Those who began upskilling even a year in advance were not only able to keep their jobs but often transitioned into higher-value positions. Meanwhile, colleagues who delayed fell behind. The AI shift isn't looming—it's here. Current adoption curves suggest that over the next three to five years, at least half of all business processes will involve AI in some form (OECD, 2025).

Getting Started: Actionable Steps

Aspiring AI engineers can take clear, proven steps to begin. Choose a learning path via Coursera, Udemy, or DataCamp that aligns with your goals. Dedicate 6 to 12 months to mastering core tools—Python, scikit-learn, TensorFlow—and apply that knowledge through real projects like classifiers, recommender systems, or computer vision apps. Publish everything on GitHub.

Engage with open-source communities to gather feedback and connect with hiring networks. Track your growth by comparing your skill set to job descriptions in your target field, adjusting your learning plan accordingly.

By taking action now, you prepare yourself for exponential opportunities. As companies and industries undergo deep, AI-powered transformation, the demand for applied, hands-on engineering talent will only grow stronger (OECD, 2025; Sharps, 2024).

Common Misconceptions: What AI Engineering Is NOT

A widespread misunderstanding about AI engineering is the belief that it mostly involves basic data handling—cleaning spreadsheets or generating simple charts. In reality, AI engineering goes far beyond routine analysis. While anyone can filter data in Excel, AI engineers design systems that automatically process, learn from, and adapt to raw inputs. Take, for instance, a full machine learning pipeline: instead of performing one-off analyses, engineers architect workflows that ingest data from multiple sources, clean and transform it, train models, validate performance, and trigger retraining automatically when new data arrives. The result isn't a static dashboard—it's a living, adaptive system that supports critical outcomes like fraud detection or personalized recommendations. Confusing surface-level data tasks with this deeper engineering work often leaves professionals stuck in roles that risk being automated by the very systems true AI engineers are building (Artificial Intelligence vs. Machine Learning | CMU, n.d.).

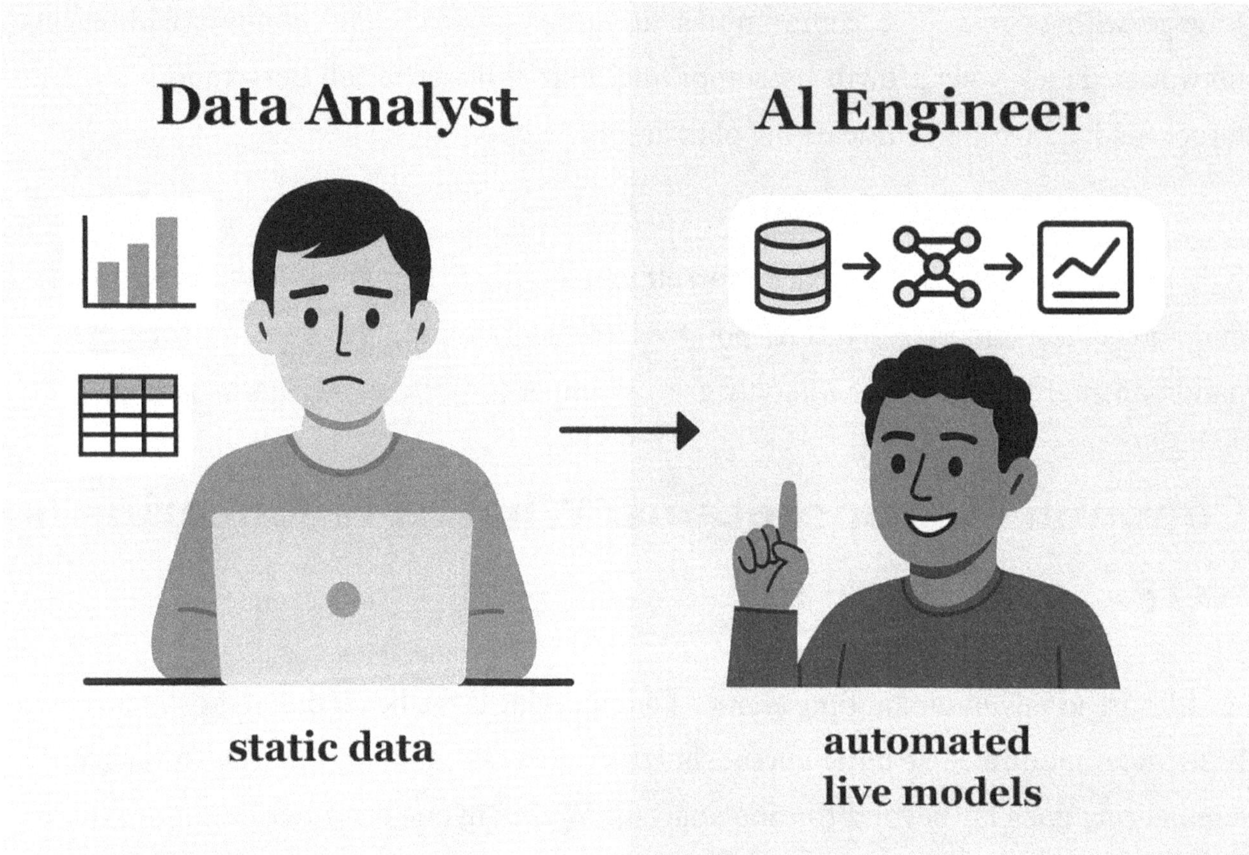

Another common mistake is equating hobbyist experimentation with real engineering. Running a few ML scripts on sample data is not the same as building robust, scalable systems. It's easy to test a new neural network architecture on a laptop, but professional systems must handle data growth—from thousands of records to billions—and scale under heavy load. Engineers must build infrastructure that supports failover, autoscaling, and real-time monitoring. Imagine designing a cloud-based image recognition service for retail: it must maintain 99.99% uptime, respond in under a second, and operate smoothly during peak sales events. Overlooking these demands leads to fragile systems, failed launches, and lost user trust (de Saint Laurent, 2018).

Many newcomers stay in the theoretical comfort zone, developing prototypes that never leave the lab. But true AI engineering is defined by deployment. It's not enough to build a recommendation engine—you need to integrate it with live inventory systems, keep it updated in real time, and monitor its effect on customer behavior. Professional-grade deployments involve version control, rollback strategies, feedback loops, and success metrics like increased conversions or reduced churn. Work that remains undeployed becomes shelfware—unused code that provides no value and limits career growth. Teams known for shipping and sustaining production systems are the ones that make visible business impact (Artificial Intelligence vs. Machine Learning | CMU, n.d.).

Finally, it's a myth that AI engineers must commit to a single tool or platform. In fact, tool agnosticism is a mark of technical maturity. Choosing the right framework—whether PyTorch for rapid prototyping, TensorFlow for production deployment, or scikit-learn for classical models—depends on the problem and context. Some solutions even combine tools, such as using ONNX for cross-platform portability. Engineers who can't evaluate or switch tools quickly often fall behind in a fast-changing field. The result: delays, inefficiencies, and projects that fail to evolve with new advances (de Saint Laurent, 2018).

These misconceptions can stall careers and hinder meaningful contributions. Staying stuck in basic analysis, overvaluing pet experiments, or avoiding deployment and tool flexibility all signal underdeveloped skills. In contrast, engineers who deliver real, adaptable AI systems—backed by metrics and user outcomes—demonstrate the kind of impact that employers recognize and reward.

Developing the Essential Problem-Solving Mindset for AI Engineering

Systems Thinking in AI Engineering

AI engineering requires a systems-oriented mindset. Successful engineers don't see their work as isolated models or tools, but as parts of a living, interconnected ecosystem of components, processes, and people. Every element—algorithms, data sources, server infrastructure, user interfaces—both shapes and is shaped by the rest. A small improvement in data quality, for instance, can ripple through a pipeline and significantly

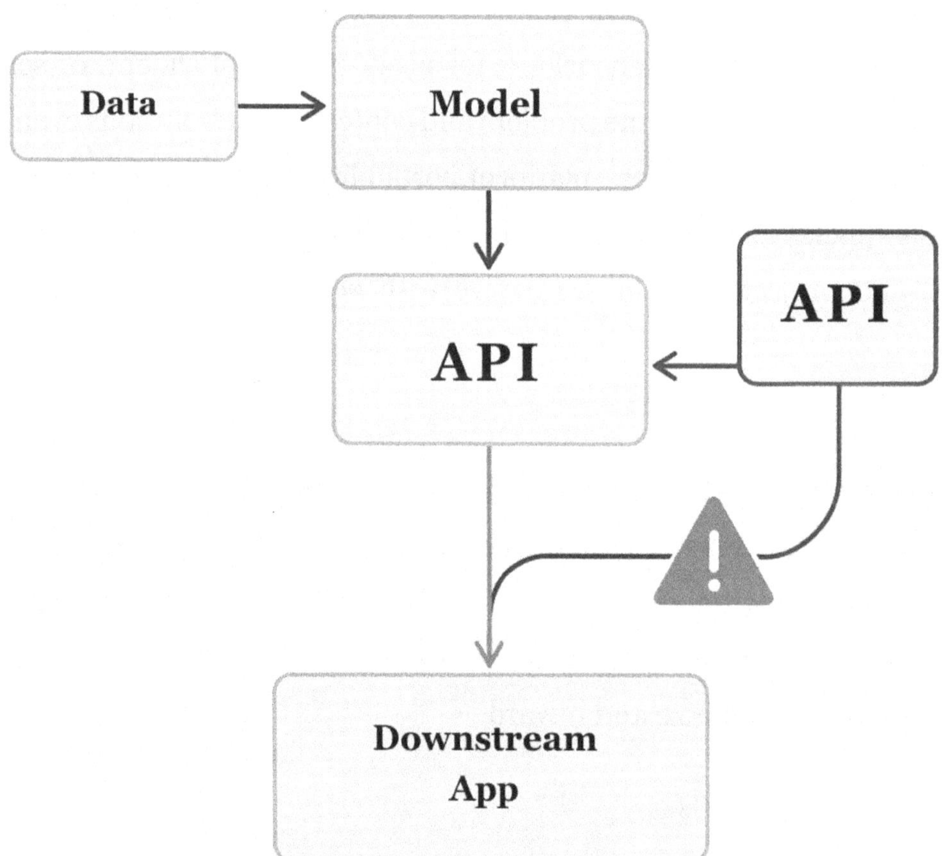

boost prediction accuracy. Conversely, a minor mismatch between a model's output format and a downstream system can break an otherwise solid solution.

In healthcare, the Cleveland Clinic applied systems thinking to analyze patient flow and uncover hidden inefficiencies caused by treatment protocols and staffing levels (Kalayjian, 2024). Local fixes—like adding nurses or rescheduling appointments—didn't reduce delays. It was only by mapping the entire patient journey that engineers designed interventions that improved outcomes across the board. AI projects follow similar patterns: a recommendation engine might seem underperforming, but the root cause may lie in inconsistent logging or misaligned update schedules. Engineers who understand the full system avoid one-off fixes and instead build resilient solutions that withstand change (Kalayjian, 2024).

This mindset is also critical at scale. At Amazon, engineers continuously gather feedback from users, devices, and internal teams, feeding it into a dynamic, system-wide knowledge loop (Kalayjian, 2024). Rather than just searching for bugs, they monitor for unexpected interactions across services. This broader awareness helps prevent short-term optimizations that lead to long-term problems and enables engineers to catch system-wide breakdowns before they escalate.

Professional Resilience and Debugging Methods

AI engineering is inherently filled with obstacles. Data inconsistencies, model instability, and environmental drift often manifest as unexpected bugs or unpredictable performance shifts. Effective engineers approach these setbacks not as roadblocks, but as valuable signals—treating each issue as an opportunity to learn and improve.

Debugging complex systems begins with decomposing failure. When a model underperforms, resilient engineers break down the problem into clear hypotheses: Is the issue due to biased data, misaligned features, or deployment errors? They test each possibility methodically, replicate errors in controlled settings, and iterate based on findings. This process is supported by rigorous practices—like versioning both code and datasets—to trace changes and uncover root causes (What Is the AI Development Lifecycle?, 2015).

When Unilever attempted to reduce its environmental impact through AI-driven supply chain optimization, early versions of the system stumbled due to flawed lifecycle data (Kalayjian, 2024). Instead of abandoning the initiative, engineers conducted thorough root cause analyses, discovered inconsistencies in supplier records, and built a tighter feedback loop. Their persistence paid off—delivering a more accurate model, improved operational reliability, and tangible cost savings.

Strong engineers grow more effective by fostering a culture where failure is openly discussed and mined for insight. A model crash in production isn't a defeat—it's a signal. It reveals where systems need hardening and where smarter design can prevent future breakdowns. In this way, every failure becomes part of a continuous learning cycle—driving stronger systems, better collaboration, and long-term resilience.

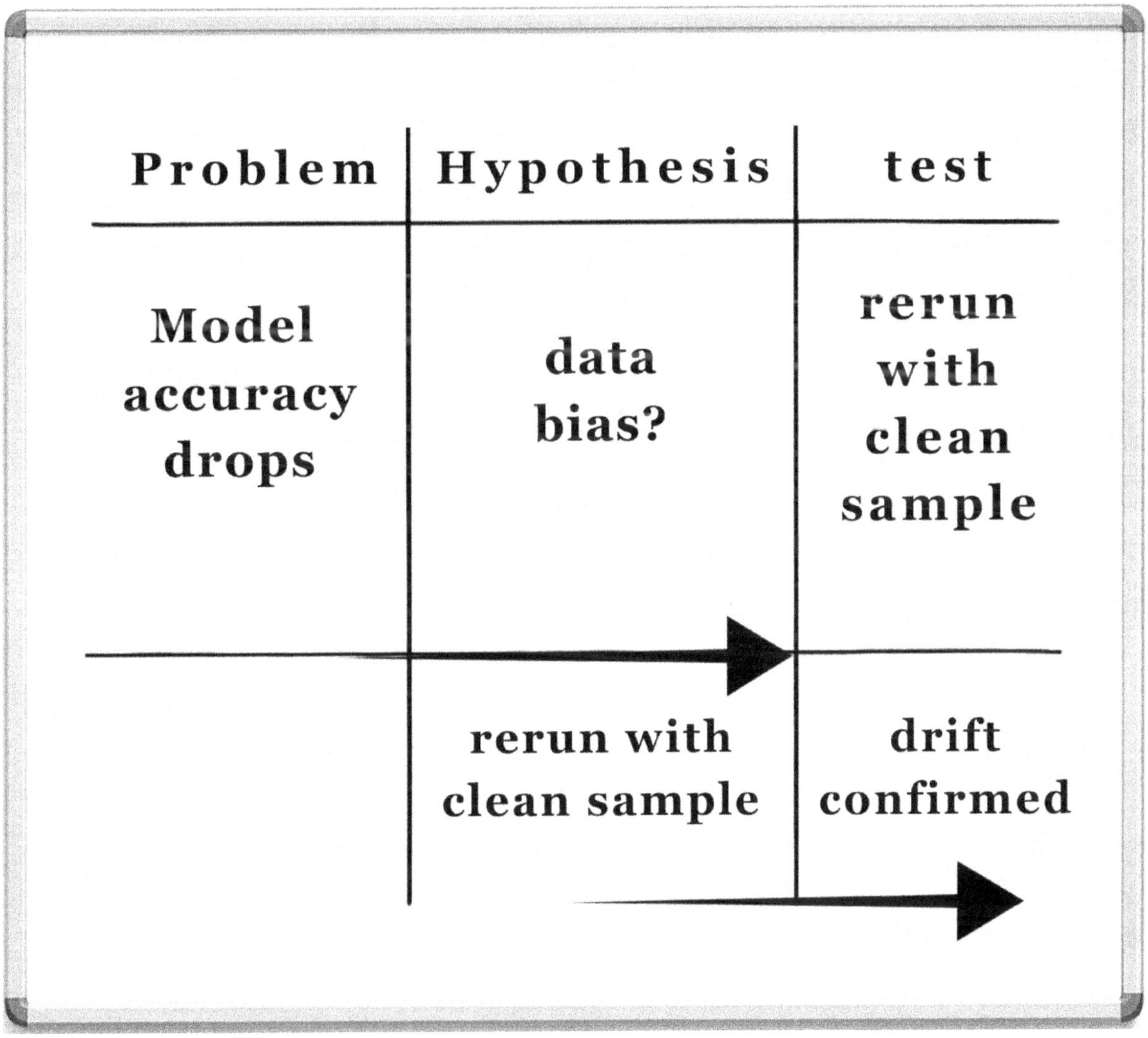

Iterative Development and Prototyping Techniques

Effective AI engineering thrives on incremental, iterative development—not big-bang launches. Instead of deploying large, untested models all at once, engineers adopt a structured cycle: define a clear problem, build a minimal viable prototype, evaluate it in a controlled environment, analyze outcomes, and refine. Each loop adds features or improves performance only when there's measurable proof that it works.

This risk-managed approach unfolds in distinct stages. It starts with well-scoped goals, followed by phased data gathering and lightweight experiments to validate key assumptions before scaling. For instance, in early cybersecurity applications of AI, engineers used targeted experiments—like static and dynamic code analysis—to uncover model weaknesses against adversarial threats, catching critical flaws long before full deployment (What Is the AI Development Lifecycle?, 2015).

Proven techniques like A/B testing or shadow deployment help evaluate new models side-by-side with existing systems, ensuring no disruption to end users. Low-fidelity prototypes often surface usability issues or integration bugs that would be expensive to fix later. This continuous, adaptive approach keeps engineering efforts lean, flexible, and aligned with fast-changing real-world environments.

A Results-Focused Engineering Approach

The most effective AI engineers anchor their work in measurable outcomes—not just effort. Success metrics are defined from the outset, typically aligning with key performance indicators (KPIs) relevant to the business context, such as model accuracy, latency, user satisfaction, or cost efficiency (What Is the AI Development Lifecycle?, 2015). Instead of counting hours or models built, they track progress against clear, results-driven targets.

To ensure alignment, engineers actively involve stakeholders to define what success truly means, then design systems that deliver on that promise. In Finland's education system, for example, AI-guided curriculum reforms weren't judged by rollout speed alone—they were evaluated through improvements in student outcomes, well-being, and retention, demonstrating real-world impact beyond the technical layer (Kalayjian, 2024).

When performance falls short, teams respond with data-driven adjustments. Engineers routinely assess whether their work is producing meaningful gains or just superficial change. In business contexts, they focus development efforts on features that directly improve customer satisfaction or hit strategic KPIs, ensuring each sprint contributes to tangible value (What Is the AI Development Lifecycle?, 2015).

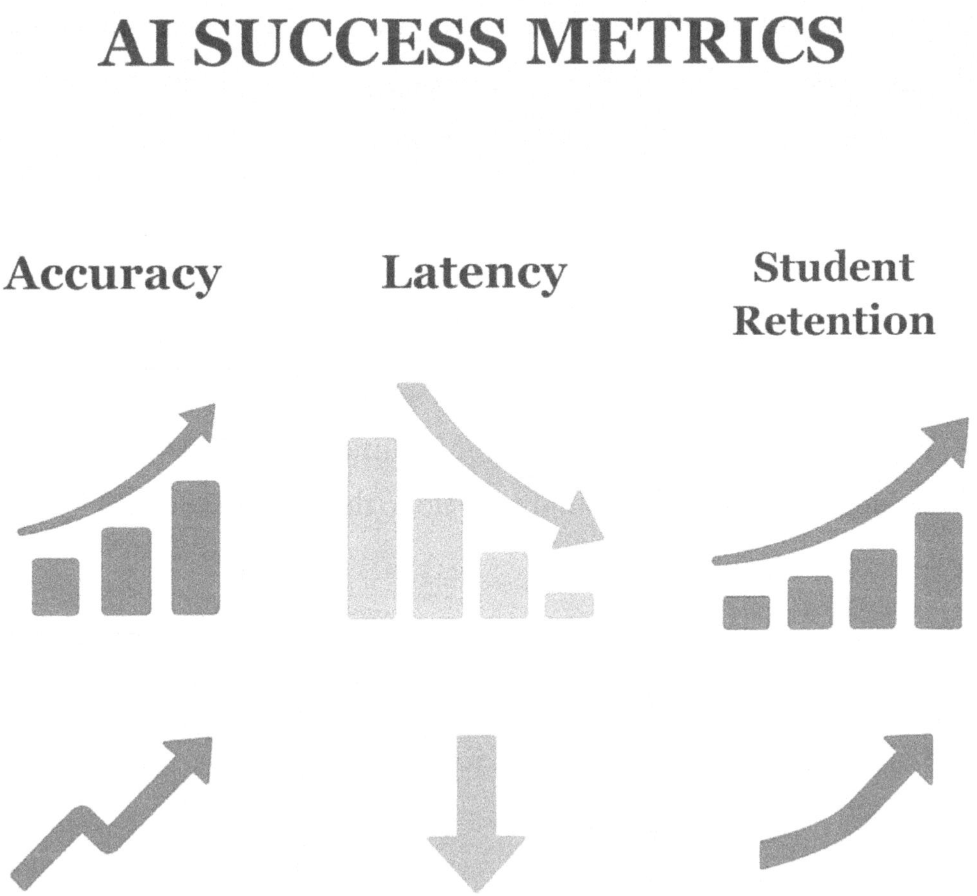

Engineers who combine systems-level thinking, professional resilience, iterative development, and an unwavering focus on outcomes are the ones who consistently build solutions that last—and adapt—in the real world.

Bringing It All Together

Now that AI engineering has been explored as a hands-on, practical discipline centered on building and deploying real-world systems, you're equipped to move forward with clarity and purpose. Mastering the intersection of coding, cloud technologies, and systems thinking empowers you to tackle complex challenges and deliver results that matter.

By shedding common misconceptions and embracing a mindset of continuous learning, collaboration, and resilience, you align yourself with the evolving demands of the industry. Focusing on functional, scalable solutions—and taking ownership from concept to deployment—helps you build a portfolio that proves your ability to turn theory into impact.

This approach sets the foundation for a thriving, future-ready career in AI engineering—one grounded in real skills, real value, and real-world outcomes.

Chapter 3
The Tools of an AI Engineer: Your Modern Stack

By 2025, AI engineering had matured into a rich yet accessible ecosystem of tools and platforms designed to streamline the creation of intelligent applications. Picture managing an AI project where every phase—data preprocessing, model training, deployment, and monitoring—flows within a cohesive, well-integrated stack. Behind every successful solution lies a toolkit of APIs that simplify tasks like natural language processing, repositories filled with customizable pre-trained models, high-performance frameworks for asynchronous APIs, container technologies that guarantee consistent environments, and experiment tracking systems that bring structure to rapid iteration.

This chapter revisits the turning point when these technologies began to converge into unified workflows that anyone with Python skills could navigate. The real challenge shifted from inventing novel algorithms to mastering the tools that translate raw ideas into reliable, scalable AI services. Whether interacting with powerful language models via simple APIs, fine-tuning community-shared models through collaborative hubs, or deploying microservices in containerized environments, engineers discovered that knowing how tools connect is as essential as the code they write.

For aspiring AI engineers, software developers entering the AI space, or tech enthusiasts eager to understand how real-world intelligent systems operate, learning this modern stack unlocks new opportunities for hands-on growth. It highlights where real innovation occurs—not just in model design, but in building the robust infrastructure and workflows that power sustainable AI products. This chapter begins your exploration of the essential components shaping today's AI engineering toolkit.

OpenAI API: Gateway to Language AI

The OpenAI API opens up a flexible and powerful suite of tools that enable developers to integrate language AI into real-world applications with minimal friction. With just a few lines of Python, you can generate human-like text, write code, translate languages, summarize content, and more—making it an ideal starting point for hands-on AI engineering.

Let's walk through how it works in practice, using Python's official openai library.

-

Text Completion

The following example shows how to use the ChatCompletion endpoint to generate a professional email:

```
def generate_email():
    import openai
    openai.api_key = "YOUR_API_KEY"

    response = openai.ChatCompletion.create(
        model="gpt-4.1",
        messages=[
            {"role": "system", "content": "You are an email
assistant."},
            {"role": "user", "content": "Draft an email to schedule a
meeting next Monday at 10AM."}
```

```
        ]
    )

    print(response['choices'][0]['message']['content'])
```

Expected output:

```
Hi, I hope this message finds you well. Would you be available to
meet next Monday at 10AM? Please let me know if that time works
for yo
```

Code Generation

You can easily switch contexts by adjusting the system prompt. Here's how to generate a function that reverses a string:

```
def generate_code():
    import openai
    openai.api_key = "YOUR_API_KEY"

    response = openai.ChatCompletion.create(
        model="gpt-4.1",
        messages=[
            {"role": "system", "content": "You are a helpful coding
assistant."},
            {"role": "user", "content": "Write a Python function to
reverse a string."}
        ]
    )
```

```
    print(response['choices'][0]['message']['content'])
```

Output:

```
def reverse_string(s):
    return s[::-1]
```

-

```
def translate_text():
    import openai
    openai.api_key = "YOUR_API_KEY"

    response = openai.ChatCompletion.create(
        model="gpt-4.1",
        messages=[
            {"role": "user", "content": "Translate 'How are you?' to
French."}
        ]
    )

    print(response['choices'][0]['message']['content'])
```

Expected result:

```
Comment ça va?
```

-

Setup Instructions

To get started:

1. Register at platform.openai.com and get your API key.
2. Install the client library:

```
pip install openai
```

3. Create your prompt using a messages array.

You can fine-tune behavior with parameters such as:

- temperature: higher values like 0.9 make output more random
- max_tokens: limits the length of the output

-

Error Handling Patterns

Robust applications include fallback logic:

```
try:
    response = openai.ChatCompletion.create(...)
except openai.error.AuthenticationError:
    print("Invalid API key.")
except openai.error.RateLimitError:
    print("Rate limit exceeded. Try again later.")
except Exception as e:
    print(f"Unexpected error: {e}")
```

-

Scaling and Optimization Tips

- Use gpt-4.1 for large context windows (up to 1 million tokens).

- Opt for o4-mini or similar smaller models for speed and budget-sensitive tasks.
- Reduce prompt size and batch requests where possible to minimize cost.

-

Real-World Use Cases

Customer Support Bot:

```
{"role": "system", "content": "You are a helpful customer support agent."}
```

Handle sessions with message histories and return succinct, helpful answers.

Marketing Content Generator:

```
{"role": "user", "content": "Create an engaging ad for a new eco-friendly water bottle."}
```

Sales Data Summarizer:

```
{"role": "user", "content": "Summarize key insights from this sales report: <paste content here>"}
```

-

Prototyping with Pretrained Models

The API enables rapid experimentation. You can:

- Test different phrasing of prompts
- Try various temperature settings
- Use instruction patterns like “Think step by step”

Best Practices Summary

- Be explicit in system roles
- Use proper error handling in production apps
- Track usage and cost with dashboards
- Apply client-side throttling for scale

-

OpenAI's API gives engineers the power to build intelligent applications quickly and efficiently. Whether you're prototyping a chatbot, analyzing documents, or generating personalized content, mastering these tools unlocks tangible, job-ready skills in AI engineering.

HuggingFace Hub: Community-Powered Machine Learning

The HuggingFace Hub is a central platform for accessible, collaborative machine learning, empowering AI engineers with rich resources, intuitive tools, and a vibrant community. Its expansive model repository provides access to over 300,000 models for NLP, computer vision, speech, and multimodal tasks. Engineers can easily tap into high-performance models like BERT for text classification, Whisper for speech-to-text, Stable Diffusion for image generation, and LLaMA 2 for conversational AI.

For instance, searching for sentiment analysis models yields hundreds of options, each annotated with clear metrics such as F1 score, accuracy, and uploader notes. A data scientist evaluating RoBERTa, DistilBERT, and ELECTRA can effortlessly compare version histories, dataset compatibility, and usage statistics to select the most suitable model for a Twitter opinion-mining project. Advanced metadata filters further streamline exploration, making it possible to navigate this vast ecosystem efficiently. With detailed model cards and transparent performance benchmarks, even small teams and solo developers can quickly access cutting-edge models (Daily Papers - Hugging Face, 2025).

The fine-tuning workflow is essential for customizing general-purpose models to specific domains. HuggingFace provides robust APIs and CLI tools that make adaptation straightforward. Using the popular transformers library, for example, fine-tuning a BERT model is simple:

```
from transformers import AutoTokenizer,
AutoModelForSequenceClassification, TrainingArguments, Trainer


model_name = "bert-base-uncased"
tokenizer = AutoTokenizer.from_pretrained(model_name)
model = AutoModelForSequenceClassification.from_pretrained(model_name)


training_args = TrainingArguments(
    output_dir="./results",
    num_train_epochs=3,
    per_device_train_batch_size=8,
    evaluation_strategy="epoch"
)


trainer = Trainer(
    model=model,
    args=training_args,
```

```
    train_dataset=my_train_dataset,
    eval_dataset=my_eval_dataset
)

trainer.train()
```

For command-line users, tools like `transformers-cli` support direct uploads and downloads, while the `accelerate` library simplifies distributed training on clusters and GPUs. Full fine-tuning is ideal when large labeled datasets are available—for example, in classifying radiology reports or ranking e-commerce search results. When data or compute is limited, engineers turn to parameter-efficient methods like LoRA, which are especially effective in domains like financial forecasting or clinical document analysis.

Empirical results reinforce this value: fine-tuning BERT on clinical texts with just 5,000 examples increased its F1 score from 0.82 to 0.91. Yet, commercial fine-tuning APIs often underperform—achieving only 37% accuracy on knowledge integration and 19% on content updates—highlighting the continued importance of community-shared scripts and datasets (Daily Papers - Hugging Face, 2025).

Open collaboration is another cornerstone of the Hub. The forums are hubs of active discussion, where users troubleshoot issues like model hallucination, tokenization bugs, and deployment bottlenecks. In one recent thread, the community diagnosed and resolved a latency spike in an image model following a version update, with a patch released collaboratively within 48 hours. Initiatives like the BigScience project—coordinating over 1,000 global contributors—produced the multilingual BLOOM model, showcasing the power of decentralized collaboration.

Community events such as hackathons, model sprints, and speaker series promote rapid learning and direct peer-to-peer exchange. The Open LLM Leaderboard, for example, motivates submissions and benchmarking of emerging models, accelerating innovation and helping developers stay aligned with the state of the art (Daily Papers - Hugging Face, 2025).

Transitioning from prototype to production is seamless with HuggingFace's integrated deployment features. Once trained or fine-tuned, models can be pushed to the Hub via Python scripts or Git-based workflows, automatically gaining versioning, documentation, and ready-to-use API endpoints. Hosting on HuggingFace Spaces allows for live demos using tools like Gradio or Streamlit, enabling real-time feedback and iteration.

For scalable inference, the platform offers HuggingFace Inference Endpoints, which auto-scale across AWS, Azure, or GCP, with GPU support and private cloud configurations. For instance, a fintech API might deploy a BART summarizer via an auto-scaling endpoint, delivering summaries in under 300 milliseconds globally. And with just one line of code—`pipeline("text-classification", model="my-model")`—developers can deploy robust inference pipelines with minimal overhead.

Backed by extensive documentation and actively maintained libraries, HuggingFace's infrastructure ensures reproducibility and stability from research to production.

By combining easy model access, efficient fine-tuning, vibrant collaboration, and frictionless deployment, HuggingFace Hub redefines the machine learning workflow and serves as an indispensable engine for modern AI development (Daily Papers - Hugging Face, 2025).

FastAPI: Lightning Fast APIs for AI

Speed and Async Capabilities

AI workloads often demand rapid, non-blocking inference delivery—whether models run locally or through platforms like HuggingFace. FastAPI, built atop Starlette and powered by Python type hints, offers asynchronous request handling at scale. Its async/await syntax allows for non-blocking I/O operations, ideal for model inference or remote data access without halting the application thread. A typical async route in FastAPI looks like:

```
from fastapi import FastAPI

app = FastAPI()

@app.post("/predict")
async def predict(data: dict):
    result = await async_model_infer(data)
    return {"prediction": result}
```

Here, `async_model_infer` might call a hosted ML model or retrieve artifacts from cloud storage. FastAPI's event loop ensures other requests are served concurrently—vital when inference latency varies under bursty loads (Service, 2024; Raman Bazhanau, 2024).

FastAPI ranks among the top-performing Python frameworks, with benchmarks showing near Node.js and Go-level throughput under ASGI servers like Uvicorn or Gunicorn with UvicornWorker. When optimized, it can handle tens of thousands of requests per second—making it well-suited for latency-sensitive AI services (Service, 2024).

Documentation Features

FastAPI automatically generates OpenAPI-compliant (Swagger) documentation based on Python type hints and Pydantic models. This enables interactive testing and streamlined integration. For example:

```
from pydantic import BaseModel

class InputData(BaseModel):
    inputs: list[str]

@app.post("/classify", response_model=dict)
async def classify(input: InputData):
    result = await model.classify(input.inputs)
    return {"outputs": result}
```

This setup produces a live Swagger UI at `/docs` and ReDoc at `/redoc`, enabling users to explore input formats and try real-time inference. Type hints reduce runtime bugs and accelerate onboarding by clearly defining expected inputs and outputs (Service, 2024; Raman Bazhanau, 2024).

Scalability Elements

FastAPI's stateless design supports scale-out architectures. For production AI endpoints—like text classifiers or vision pipelines—multiple workers can run under Gunicorn using:

```
# gunicorn.conf.py
workers = 4
worker_class = "uvicorn.workers.UvicornWorker"
```

Adding Nginx as a reverse proxy provides SSL termination, static asset delivery, and efficient routing. A robust production stack might include:

- FastAPI app with async model inference
- Uvicorn or Gunicorn (ASGI server)
- Systemd or Supervisor for process management
- Nginx for reverse proxy and SSL
- Optional CDN for ML artifact delivery

FastAPI is widely adopted in containerized environments (e.g., Docker, Kubernetes), supporting blue-green deployments, rolling updates, and autoscaling—essential for continuously evolving ML models (Service, 2024; Raman Bazhanau, 2024).

Microservices and Integration Patterns

FastAPI embraces microservice principles, enabling inference endpoints to act as independent services. These can communicate via REST, WebSockets, or gRPC and integrate with model registries, observability platforms, and security layers.

Testing Framework

For robust development, FastAPI provides a TestClient for simulating API calls:

```
from fastapi.testclient import TestClient

client = TestClient(app)

def test_classify():
    response = client.post("/classify", json={"inputs": ["example
text"]})
    assert response.status_code == 200
    assert "outputs" in response.json()
```

This supports unit and integration testing with ease. Exception handlers and built-in logging accelerate debugging, while native support for Prometheus and ELK stacks enables detailed monitoring (Raman Bazhanau, 2024).

FastAPI's use of environment variables, structured logs, and container-friendly architecture ensures smooth integration into CI/CD pipelines and DevOps workflows.

Together, HuggingFace and FastAPI offer a powerful stack for building, fine-tuning, serving, and scaling AI solutions with speed, reliability, and developer-friendly tooling.

Scalability Elements

FastAPI's stateless design supports scale-out architectures. For production AI endpoints—like text classifiers or vision pipelines—multiple workers can run under Gunicorn using:

```
# gunicorn.conf.py
workers = 4
worker_class = "uvicorn.workers.UvicornWorker"
```

Adding Nginx as a reverse proxy provides SSL termination, static asset delivery, and efficient routing. A robust production stack might include:

- FastAPI app with async model inference
- Uvicorn or Gunicorn (ASGI server)
- Systemd or Supervisor for process management
- Nginx for reverse proxy and SSL
- Optional CDN for ML artifact delivery

FastAPI is widely adopted in containerized environments (e.g., Docker, Kubernetes), supporting blue-green deployments, rolling updates, and autoscaling—essential for continuously evolving ML models (Service, 2024; Raman Bazhanau, 2024).

Microservices and Integration Patterns

FastAPI embraces microservice principles, enabling inference endpoints to act as independent services. These can communicate via REST, WebSockets, or gRPC and integrate with model registries, observability platforms, and security layers.

Testing Framework

For robust development, FastAPI provides a TestClient for simulating API calls:

```
from fastapi.testclient import TestClient

client = TestClient(app)

def test_classify():
    response = client.post("/classify", json={"inputs": ["example
text"]})
    assert response.status_code == 200
    assert "outputs" in response.json()
```

This supports unit and integration testing with ease. Exception handlers and built-in logging accelerate debugging, while native support for Prometheus and ELK stacks enables detailed monitoring (Raman Bazhanau, 2024).

FastAPI's use of environment variables, structured logs, and container-friendly architecture ensures smooth integration into CI/CD pipelines and DevOps workflows.

Together, HuggingFace and FastAPI offer a powerful stack for building, fine-tuning, serving, and scaling AI solutions with speed, reliability, and developer-friendly tooling.

Docker: Reliable Deployment Everywhere

Docker has become a cornerstone for AI engineers seeking effortless deployment and robust reproducibility. AI projects depend on a complex web of frameworks, system libraries, and hardware drivers, making consistent environments difficult to reproduce. Docker's core advantage lies in packaging all software dependencies—Python, CUDA drivers, TensorFlow, PyTorch, scikit-learn, and datasets—into self-contained, portable images.

By defining a Dockerfile, engineers can lock down every component, including base operating system versions. A typical AI Dockerfile might begin with `python:3.8-slim`, install dependencies with `pip install -r requirements.txt`, copy over custom binaries, and set critical environment variables like `CUDA_VISIBLE_DEVICES`. The result is an immutable container that behaves identically whether running on a laptop, GPU cluster, or cloud node (Vidya Ugare, 2024).

Reproducibility is especially vital in research and regulated domains. Docker makes the entire build process explicit. Instead of manually configuring a new machine, a teammate can run:

```
docker build .
docker run -it <image>
```

...and spin up an identical environment in seconds. This ensures compatibility when precise versions of TensorFlow or CUDA are required. NVIDIA integration is handled using CUDA base images and the `nvidia-docker` runtime to enable GPU support across training and inference. This eliminates environment drift and accelerates the transition from experimentation to production (Breaking down the Web Application Deployment Process, n.d.).

Managing container versions over time is critical as models and dependencies evolve. Docker supports image tagging—e.g., `1.0.0`, `experiment-20240120`, or `latest`. Teams can track, reproduce, and roll back configurations. Dependencies are typically pinned in `requirements.txt`, and descriptive tags (like `ml-model-cuda112-torch180`) are used when pushing to registries. This versioned history ensures that previous environments can be redeployed instantly if regressions appear.

When updates are needed—like upgrading PyTorch or adding a preprocessing script—a new image is built and stored, never overwriting existing builds. Teams can quickly switch between versions, restoring functionality or reproducing bugs with precision (Vidya Ugare, 2024).

For collaboration, Docker registries serve as centralized distribution points. Public options like Docker Hub and private solutions such as AWS Elastic Container Registry allow teams to `docker push` and `docker pull` shared environments. This guarantees that all contributors use the same configurations, eliminating environment inconsistencies. Debugging becomes systematic: if a bug only appears on a colleague's machine, it can be reproduced exactly using the shared image (Breaking down the Web Application Deployment Process, n.d.; Vidya Ugare, 2024).

When scaling beyond development machines, Docker integrates seamlessly with major cloud providers. AWS, Azure, and GCP natively support container deployment. Platforms like AWS SageMaker or Google AI Platform accept Docker images directly as inference endpoints. In production, containers are typically orchestrated by Kubernetes, which automates horizontal scaling, fault recovery, and traffic routing.

A common CI/CD pipeline might:

- Train a model in GitHub Actions
- Build a Docker image on successful commit
- Push it to a registry
- Automatically update running services with the new image

This enables zero-downtime updates for AI models, inference scripts, and dependency changes. Docker thus transforms AI deployment from a manual, error-prone process into a streamlined, automated lifecycle (Vidya Ugare, 2024; Breaking down the Web Application Deployment Process, n.d.).

MLflow: Monitoring AI in the Wild

Containerized environments have become standard in AI engineering, delivering consistency and scalability for building, training, and deploying machine learning models. Within these environments, managing a growing number of experiments, datasets, and models can quickly become chaotic. MLflow addresses this complexity by unifying experiment tracking, metric logging, reproducibility, and visualization, empowering teams to maintain rigorous control over ML workflows while accelerating development. By integrating natively with major ML libraries and supporting flexible deployment options, MLflow enables seamless adoption across varied technical stacks and organizational contexts (MLflow: A Tool for Managing the Machine Learning Lifecycle | MLflow, 2025

MLflow: Managing the Machine Learning Lifecycle

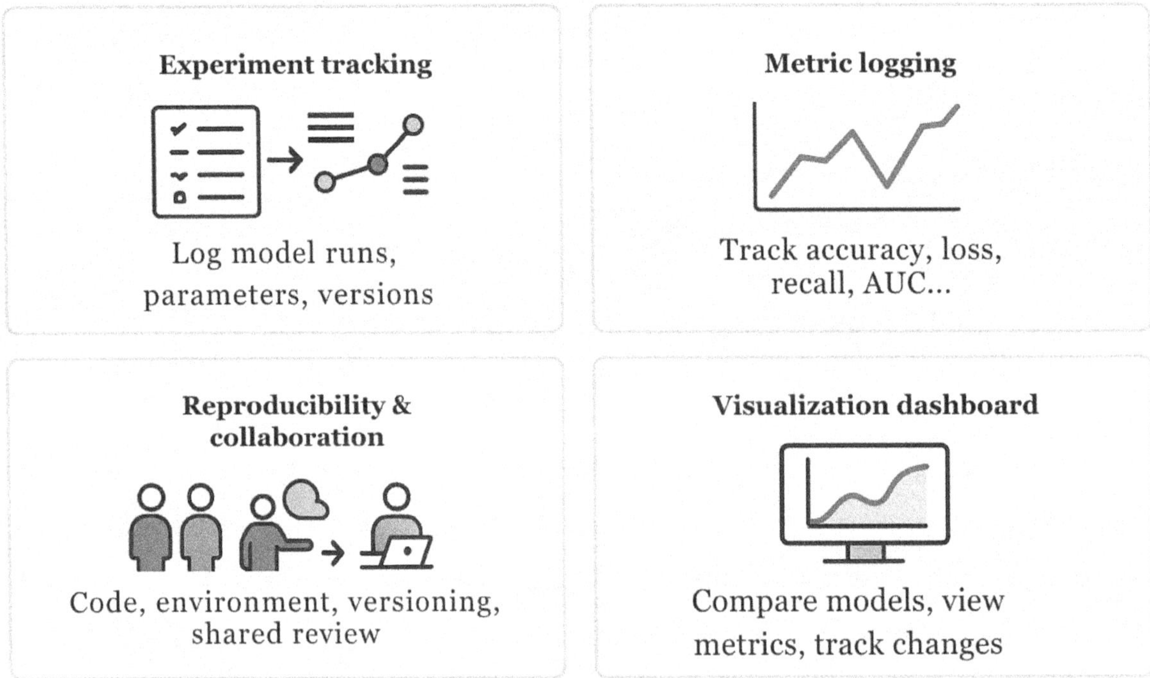

Machine learning projects often require running dozens or even hundreds of experiments to tune hyperparameters and improve model performance. MLflow's experiment tracking allows developers to log each training run with all relevant parameters, artifacts, model code, and results. For instance, when training a scikit-learn regression model, an engineer would track input features, model type, regularization parameters, random seed, git commit SHA, and even the environment's Python version. These parameters are logged automatically with `mlflow.autolog()` or manually for greater customization, building a complete archive of every attempt (MLflow, 2025).

Suppose a data scientist wants to compare random forests with different depths and learning rates: by logging each run, all variations—model structure, training data split, and results—are stored for later comparison. Model comparison becomes intuitive, as MLflow presents side-by-side tables of runs, allowing the most promising models based on validation accuracy, loss, or F1 score to be easily identified. If a run produces poor results due to a bad parameter or a data bug, the corresponding log enables rapid root cause analysis.

Metric Logging

Tracking precise performance metrics is essential for diagnosing the health of experiments and the quality of model outputs. MLflow supports automatic or custom metric logging, allowing practitioners to monitor standard metrics like accuracy, precision, recall, loss, and ROC-AUC, while also capturing domain-specific indicators. These metrics are updated in real time and stored for every experiment.

ML engineers can set up alerts to monitor warning signs, such as a sudden spike in loss, vanishing gradients, or metric plateaus indicating overfitting or data drift. Automated logging greatly decreases manual errors and provides a reliable metric history. When tuning models, observing convergence curves and metric fluctuations helps pinpoint effective hyperparameters. For example, a steep accuracy drop-off after increasing model complexity would suggest overfitting—a scenario instantly visible in the MLflow UI (MLflow, 2025).

Reproducibility and Collaboration

Reproducibility is a constant challenge in AI development, especially when code, data, and dependencies are updated frequently or team members contribute remote changes. MLflow addresses this by logging every necessary component: parameter values, model code, weights, dependencies, versioned artifacts, and data samples, ensuring any run can be restored precisely.

The environment configuration, including installed libraries and system-level prerequisites, is logged via MLflow's environment tracking features. This makes it possible to recreate experiments, audit production models, and satisfy compliance requirements for regulated industries. For example, a model trained on one engineer's laptop can be replicated by a teammate working in cloud containers because MLflow captures the conda or pip environment in use and the script that launched the run.

Successful team collaboration is facilitated by shared MLflow servers, enabling multiple users to review, comment, and promote model versions through systematic stages, such as staging, production, and archiving (MLflow: A Tool for Managing the Machine Learning Lifecycle | MLflow, 2025).

Visualization Capabilities

Visualizing data is key to insight and decision-making. The MLflow dashboard offers progress tracking, metric plotting, and model artifact browsing. Users can interpret performance charts—like accuracy-over-time traces, parameter heatmaps, and confusion matrices—to guide model selection and iteration.

Comparing dozens of model runs, each with varying input data or architectures, is simplified to a few dashboard clicks. Performance degradations, outlier runs, and optimization convergences become instantly apparent. When an engineer presents results to stakeholders, MLflow's visualizations provide clear, data-driven rationales for promoting selected models to production or retraining them on fresh data.

Setting up MLflow in a basic deep learning workflow might involve launching an MLflow tracking server in a Docker container, instrumenting training scripts using `mlflow.autolog()`, and examining results via the UI. A common pitfall is failing to synchronize version control with experiment tracking, resulting in "lost" model context; this is mitigated by logging git SHA with each run, a best practice for auditability.

Effective team collaboration happens when all members contribute to a shared MLflow instance, annotate promising runs, and review registered models through an approval workflow, reducing friction and enabling consistent, reproducible data science at scale (MLflow, 2025).

By embedding MLflow into containerized workflows, organizations bring lasting order, traceability, and reliability to AI engineering processes.

Bringing It All Together

Now that we have explored the essential tools and platforms shaping modern AI engineering—from leveraging powerful language model APIs and community-driven resources to building scalable APIs with FastAPI, deploying reliable environments using Docker, and effectively tracking experiments with MLflow—you are equipped with a practical foundation to build, deploy, and manage AI applications confidently.

Mastering these technologies enables you to move beyond theory into hands-on development, creating solutions that perform reliably in real-world settings while maintaining reproducibility and scalability. As you continue your learning journey, integrating these tools will accelerate your ability to deliver impactful AI projects, adapt to evolving demands, and contribute meaningfully to the vibrant, collaborative AI engineering community.

Chapter 4

Chatbot Wizardry: Building Your First AI Project with OpenAI

Have you ever wondered what it takes to create an AI chatbot that feels natural and helpful rather than robotic and confusing? How do developers turn a simple idea into a working program that understands conversations, responds appropriately, and grows smarter over time?

What tools and steps are needed to build a chatbot using OpenAI's technology, from setting up the coding environment to refining its responses and presenting the final project professionally?

If these questions have crossed your mind, this chapter offers a clear path through the process. It will guide you in crafting your first AI chatbot by breaking down each stage—from designing user-friendly conversations and preparing your development setup to writing code, testing performance, and expanding capabilities.

Along the way, you'll discover practical methods to ensure your chatbot handles real-world interactions smoothly and learn how to showcase your work effectively for future opportunities. Whether you're starting out in AI engineering, transitioning as a software developer, or simply curious about building intelligent applications, this chapter lays the foundation for creating functional, reliable chatbots with confidence.

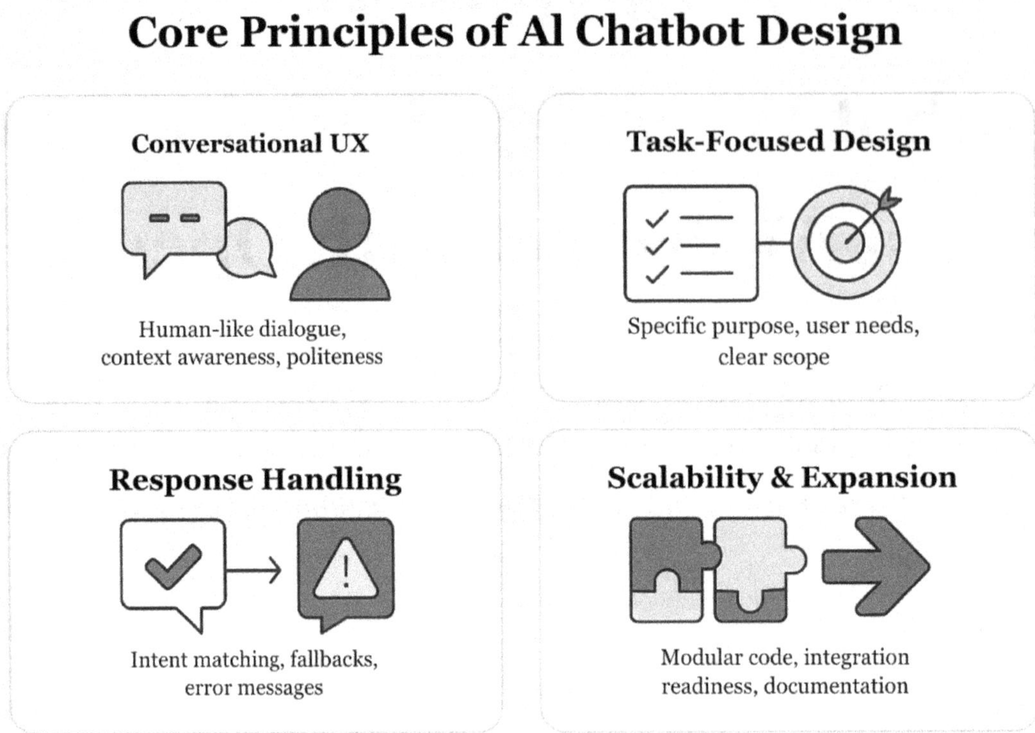

Laying the Foundation: Chatbot Design Principles

A well-designed chatbot begins with a deep understanding of conversational user experience (UX). At its core, natural interaction requires conversation flows that mimic authentic human dialogue—accounting for context, turn-taking, and language that feels intuitive. Trust is reinforced through thoughtful design elements like polite greetings, relevant responses, and transparency about the bot's capabilities.

For instance, a chatbot that begins with "Hello, how can I help you today?" and presents clear options reflects user-centric thinking. In contrast, bots that ignore user context or respond robotically erode trust quickly. Effective conversational structures acknowledge queries, ask clarifying questions when needed, and provide confirmations or follow-ups.

A travel assistant, for example, builds user confidence by clearly confirming flight selections and travel policies (Janssen et al., 2022; Amore Rossouw & Smuts, 2023).

Good UX design goes beyond simple exchanges. Techniques such as politeness strategies, guided prompts, and defined boundaries help users feel respected and in control. For older adults, phrasing instructions as suggestions—rather than commands—fosters comfort and aligns with politeness theory (Amore Rossouw & Smuts, 2023). Transparency also matters: clearly stating, "I'm an AI assistant and cannot offer legal advice, but I can help you find resources," builds trust and sets expectations (Janssen et al., 2022).

The next design pillar is task-focused functionality. A chatbot should launch with a clearly defined purpose rooted in real user needs. This begins with stakeholder interviews and journey mapping to identify which problems the bot will solve and which should be escalated or redirected. For example, an e-commerce support bot should prioritize core functions like order tracking, returns, and product FAQs, rather than handling unrelated requests.

A well-scoped project aligns the chatbot's task boundaries with practical outcomes and available resources. Developers should define initial intents and actions clearly, enabling user feedback to guide future iterations (Janssen et al., 2022). Narrow, focused scopes tend to outperform broad ones in terms of clarity and user satisfaction.

Another critical principle is robust response handling. Validating chatbot outputs helps ensure relevance and clarity. Key techniques include context tracking and accurate intent matching. When uncertainty arises, fallback responses like "I'm not sure how to help with that—would you like to speak to a person?" provide graceful exits without overpromising.

Transparent error handling reinforces trust. Instead of cryptic messages, bots should rephrase prompts or offer suggestions. For example: "I didn't catch that. You can ask me about product details or shipping." This keeps users on track and prevents conversational dead ends (Amore Rossouw & Smuts, 2023; Janssen et al., 2022).

Planning for expansion is the final pillar. Modular architecture allows developers to add new features—like greetings, support flows, or integrations—without breaking existing components. Each intent should be built as an independent module to support maintainability and agile updates.

Comprehensive documentation is key for scaling: mapping intents, responses, and API connections ensures smooth onboarding and debugging. Integration readiness is also crucial, as chatbots often connect to CRMs, payment systems, or analytics platforms. API-driven design supports data fetching, real-time updates, and multilingual support.

Together, these design principles—conversational UX, task-focused structure, response handling, and modular scalability—provide a framework for building reliable, user-friendly chatbots. Grounded in practical research, they ensure your chatbot evolves with user needs while maintaining clarity, consistency, and trust (Janssen et al., 2022; Amore Rossouw & Smuts, 2023).

Setting Up for Success: Creating Your Coding Environment

Getting the development environment right is critical for building an effective and secure OpenAI-powered chatbot. This phase transforms conceptual chatbot design into tangible, maintainable code. A robust setup ensures every conversational feature and UX detail discussed earlier can be implemented and expanded smoothly.

Start by confirming that Python is installed and up to date. Open a terminal and run:

```
python --version
```

or on some systems:

```
python3 --version
```

For projects using modern frameworks like pygpt-net, Python 3.9 or higher is required. If the terminal confirms a version ≥3.9, you're good to go. On Windows, you may need to update your PATH after installing Python. Linux users can install Python 3.9+ with:

```
sudo apt-get install python3.9
```

On macOS, Homebrew is typically used:

```
brew install python@3.9
```

Python projects benefit from virtual environments to isolate dependencies. First, create a folder for your project, then set up the environment with:

```
python -m venv venv
```

or:

```
python3.9 -m venv venv
```

To activate the environment:

- On **Windows**:

```
venv\Scripts\activate
```

- On **macOS/Linux**:

```
source venv/bin/activate
```

Your prompt will show `(venv)` to confirm it's active. If activation fails, double-check paths and terminal permissions.

Next, configure secure integration with OpenAI's API. After signing in to your OpenAI account, generate an API key from the dashboard. Save this key securely—it must never be hardcoded or exposed in public code.

To store it safely:

- On **macOS/Linux**, add to your shell config (e.g., `~/.bashrc` or `~/.zshrc`):

```
export OPENAI_API_KEY='sk-xxxxxxxxxxxxxxxxxxxxxxxx'
```

- On **Windows**, in Command Prompt:

```
set OPENAI_API_KEY=sk-xxxxxxxxxxxxxxxxxxxxxxxx
```

Or use the Environment Variables menu for persistent configuration. Access the key in code via:

```
import os
api_key = os.environ["OPENAI_API_KEY"]
```

Now install the necessary packages. Use a `requirements.txt` file in your project root:

```
openai>=0.27.0
streamlit>=1.20
tiktoken
pygpt-net
```

Install all dependencies with:

```
pip install -r requirements.txt
```

If pip fails, try upgrading:

```
python -m pip install --upgrade pip
```

Then verify the setup in a Python shell:

```
import openai
import streamlit
import tiktoken
```

If no errors appear, your environment is ready.

This setup ensures reliability, modularity, and security—isolated dependencies, protected API keys, and version-controlled tooling prepare you for scalable, maintainable chatbot development. With these foundations in place, you're ready to dive into core functionality like response generation, input handling, and contextual memory (Pygpt-Net, 2023; GeeksforGeeks, 2024).

Hands-On Guide: Step-by-Step Chatbot Coding Tutorial

AI chatbots are making digital interactions smoother—whether it's answering a customer's question or guiding an employee through onboarding. Building a reliable, responsive chatbot involves a series of technical and practical steps that ensure the system is helpful and robust.

The process begins with selecting the right tools. Python is an excellent choice due to its ecosystem of NLP libraries. Packages like ChatterBot provide an easy way to launch conversational bots by training them on either pre-existing language corpora or custom datasets. With just a few lines of code, you can initialize a chatbot, train it, and start handling simple conversations:

```
from chatterbot import ChatBot
from chatterbot.trainers import ChatterBotCorpusTrainer

bot = ChatBot("HelperBot")
trainer = ChatterBotCorpusTrainer(bot)
trainer.train("chatterbot.corpus.english")
```

This setup allows your bot to understand basic interactions after minimal training (Building an AI Chatbot Using Python and NLP, 2024).

To handle real-world use cases, context management is essential. By storing conversation history, chatbots can deliver responses that align with previous interactions. This avoids repetitive questions and makes replies feel more human. For instance, if a user has already submitted their account number, the bot should avoid asking again (Building a Conversational Chatbot with GPT-4: Step-By-Step Guide, 2024).

Connecting the bot to external APIs adds utility. Whether fetching stock prices or checking inventory, real-time integrations enhance the chatbot's capabilities. Robust error handling must be implemented so the bot can gracefully inform users when data sources are unavailable.

Another key configuration is fine-tuning output parameters. Adjusting settings like temperature controls the creativity of responses. In high-precision domains like finance or HR, a lower temperature produces more focused replies; in sales or support, a higher setting may allow for friendlier, dynamic exchanges.

For advanced capabilities, consider Retrieval-Augmented Generation (RAG) and frameworks like Rasa. RAG enhances chatbots by pairing language models with knowledge retrieval systems, enabling detailed, context-aware answers from large datasets. Rasa supports structured flows, intent recognition, and multi-turn dialogues. You can define intents, entities, and stories to guide conversations with precision:

```
stories:
- story: greet and inquire product
  steps:
  - intent: greet
  - action: utter_greet
  - intent: ask_product
  - action: action_lookup_product
```

These tools support enterprise-grade bot development with extensibility and deep integration options (Building an AI Chatbot Using Python and NLP, 2024).

Real-world applications demonstrate chatbot value across sectors:

- **Customer support**: Bots handle FAQs instantly, reducing ticket volume.
- **Finance**: Assist users through eligibility checks or application steps.
- **HR**: Guide new employees through onboarding processes.
- **Sales**: Recommend products based on interaction history.
- **Internal support**: Direct staff to relevant IT or documentation resources.

Challenges remain, such as gracefully handling unexpected input, integrating multiple APIs, and maintaining data privacy. Continuous retraining ensures the bot evolves with user behavior. Cloud deployment, CI/CD pipelines, and web interfaces can streamline testing and scaling.

AI chatbots are increasingly becoming critical tools across industries. Their ability to understand, recall, connect, and automate makes them powerful allies in creating responsive, intelligent systems (Building a Conversational Chatbot with GPT-4: Step-By-Step Guide, 2024; Building an AI Chatbot Using Python and NLP, 2024).

Refining and Growing: Testing and Expanding the Chatbot

A robust approach to testing and expanding your chatbot begins with functional testing. Specific test cases should include greeting recognition, handling out-of-domain inputs, API data retrieval, escalation triggers, and multi-turn conversation handling. Your test suite should cover expected user intents, edge cases, typos, ambiguous phrasing, and adversarial inputs. Manual testing is critical, but automation greatly enhances scalability and consistency. Tools like Botium or Test My Bot help simulate user flows, validate NLP accuracy, and stress-test performance under load (SmythOS, 2024).

Structure your tests using YAML or JSON, defining user inputs, expected outputs, and assertions. This approach supports repeatability and easy test expansion. To monitor behavior and performance, implement structured logging. Record each session with timestamps, user input, predicted intent, response, and confidence scores. Here's a logging example:

```
import logging
logging.basicConfig(filename='chatbot_sessions.log',
level=logging.INFO)

def log_exchange(session_id, user_input, predicted_intent, response,
confidence):

logging.info(f"{session_id},{user_input},{predicted_intent},{confidenc
e},{response}")
```

For analytics, track metrics such as intent match accuracy, false positives/negatives, resolution rate, and response time. Build dashboards to visualize daily success rates, escalation frequency, and misunderstood phrases.

Context management remains central. Store conversation history per session, ideally within a 5–10 message window to balance coherence and API token limits. Trim or summarize history dynamically when necessary:

```
conversation_history = []

def add_to_history(role, message):
    conversation_history.append((role, message))
    if len(conversation_history) > 10:
        conversation_history.pop(0)
```

Include context reset triggers like "/reset" or auto-reset after sensitive tasks, authentication, or timeouts.

Role-based responses offer personalization and domain control. Define personas with constraints on tone, allowed topics, and response style:

```
support_persona = {
    "name": "SupportBot",
    "tone": "professional",
    "allowed_topics": ["troubleshooting", "account"],
    "response_length": "concise"
}

friendly_persona = {
    "name": "Chloe",
    "tone": "casual, friendly",
    "allowed_topics": "all",
    "response_length": "detailed"
}
```

Switch personas dynamically:

```
def set_persona(persona_name):
    global active_persona
    if persona_name == "Support":
        active_persona = support_persona
    elif persona_name == "Friendly":
        active_persona = friendly_persona
```

This influences the bot's behavior and style. For example: "Hi! How can I help you fix your problem today?" vs. "Hey there! 😊 What can I help with?"

To improve continuously, collect feedback through buttons (👍/👎), ratings, or comments. Log feedback with session links:

```
def record_feedback(session_id, rating, comment=None):
    with open('feedback.csv', 'a') as f:
        f.write(f"{session_id},{rating},{comment}\n")
```

Use this data to fine-tune classifiers, revise responses, and track satisfaction over time. Visualize metrics like satisfaction score trends or resolution improvements post-deployment.

Finally, implement a feedback-driven development loop: rerun tests after updates, analyze logs for issues, and refine models based on real-world usage. This iterative process ensures your chatbot grows more accurate, user-friendly, and adaptable over time (SmythOS, 2024; Botable Blog, 2025).

Showcasing Your Work: Presenting the Chatbot Project Professionally

Effective documentation can transform your chatbot into a polished portfolio piece. Begin with a clear and informative `README.md` file:

1. **Project Overview**: Explain what your chatbot does and its purpose.

   "This AI-powered customer support chatbot answers FAQs and routes complex queries to human agents, reducing response time and improving satisfaction."

2. **Key Features**: List capabilities clearly:

- Intent recognition
- Multi-turn conversation support
- Context-aware responses
- API integration for escalation

3. **Installation Instructions:**

```
git clone https://github.com/yourusername/chatbot-wizard.git
cd chatbot-wizard
python3 -m venv env && source env/bin/activate
pip install -r requirements.txt
```

4. **Setup:**

- Add your OpenAI API key to `.env`
- Required Python version: 3.8+
- Compatible OS: Linux, macOS, Windows

5. **Usage:**

```
python main.py
```

6. **Technical Stack:**

- Frameworks: FastAPI, Flask, React
- Databases: PostgreSQL, SQLite
- Integrations: OpenAI API, Slack, Twilio

7. **Challenges & Solutions:**

- "Handled ambiguous queries using fallback intents."
- "Reduced latency via input pre-processing and cloud deployment."

8. **Visual Demonstrations:**

- Add a screencast (2–3 minutes)
- Include animated GIFs for features like order tracking or error handling

9. **Security Measures:**

- API tokens via environment variables
- Input sanitization
- Authentication failure logging

10. **Growth Areas:**

- Add sentiment detection
- Expand to multilingual support

11. **Repository Structure**:

```
├── README.md
├── LICENSE
├── src/
│   ├── chatbot.py
│   ├── utils.py
```

```
├── tests/
│   └── test_chatbot.py
├── docs/
│   └── user_guide.md
├── deploy/
│   └── Dockerfile
```

Use clear branches: `main` (stable), `dev` (active), `feature/*`. Use descriptive commits and issue linking.

Finally, ensure every function has a docstring, major files have headers, and licensing is defined. This level of professionalism signals production-readiness and strong development practices (How to Contribute to Open-Source Projects, 2023; Interactive Programs, 2020).

Bringing It All Together

Now that you've learned the essential principles of chatbot design, set up a secure and efficient development environment, followed detailed coding steps, and explored testing, expansion, and professional presentation techniques, you are equipped to build AI chatbots that are both functional and scalable. This foundation enables you to create user-focused solutions that handle real-world challenges while maintaining reliability and adaptability. Moving forward, you can apply these skills to develop more sophisticated chatbots, integrate advanced features, and continuously improve your projects based on user feedback and evolving technology, positioning yourself confidently as a capable AI engineer or developer in this dynamic field.

Chapter 5
Going Deeper : Fine-Tuning AI with HuggingFace

Artificial intelligence models often come pretrained on broad datasets designed to handle a wide range of tasks. While these foundational models provide a powerful starting point, they may struggle when applied to specialized or domain-specific problems. Generic AI can miss subtle nuances found in technical jargon, industry-specific terms, or regulatory language, limiting accuracy and usefulness in real-world applications. This gap creates challenges for organizations seeking tailored solutions that respond precisely to their unique data and workflows.

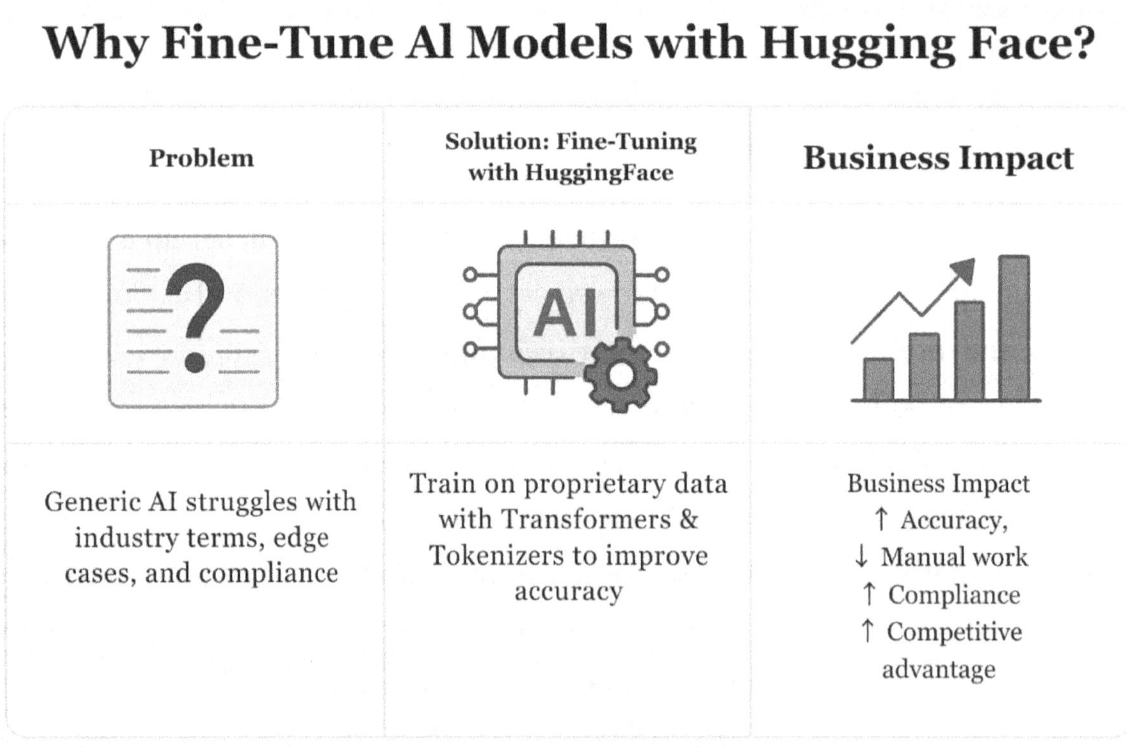

This chapter guides you through the process of fine-tuning AI models using HuggingFace tools to overcome such limitations. It begins by establishing the groundwork—selecting appropriate datasets, setting up libraries, and preparing notebooks to create an effective development environment. From there, it moves into practical training techniques, including choosing pretrained models, configuring hyperparameters, and managing tokenization and dataset splits. The chapter also covers methods for evaluating and improving your models with metrics, cross-validation, and error analysis. Finally, it emphasizes best practices for documenting and sharing your fine-tuned models, ensuring reproducibility and collaboration. Together, these steps form a clear, hands-on path toward building customized AI solutions that align closely with specific business needs and technical requirements.

Why Fine-Tuning? Targeted AI That Works

Enterprise AI adoption often confronts the limitations of general-purpose pre-trained language models. Take text classification in medical records or compliance documents: off-the-shelf models underperform on edge cases due to their lack of specialized terminology, abbreviations, or regulatory nuances. Generic language models typically misinterpret clinical shorthand or unique document structures, resulting in errors or unreliable classifications. In the financial sector, customer emails containing institution-specific phrasing or references to niche products can fall outside the typical training distribution, yielding lower accuracy and prompting labor-intensive manual review. Industry metrics show that while an unmodified foundation model might achieve 80% accuracy on domain-specific text, fine-tuning with domain data can boost performance to over 93% in challenging edge cases—a nearly 16% gain where accuracy is critical (AI Fine Tuned Models Strategy, 2025).

Fine-tuning addresses these issues by retraining underlying model weights on proprietary datasets that reflect the specific linguistic quirks, operational workflows, and regulatory contexts of an enterprise. For instance, customizing named entity recognition for an insurance provider equips the model to accurately identify company-specific policy identifiers, claims processes, or specialized clauses. In machine translation for technical manuals, incorporating domain glossaries and formatting conventions limits misinterpretation, reducing costly post-editing work. The HuggingFace Transformers library, with its Trainer API and dataset integration, enables developers to structure edge case data as supervised examples, systematically improving model behavior on previously problematic inputs.

Another critical benefit involves control and ownership of training data. By leveraging proprietary information assets—unique business lexicons, customer histories, and confidential process records—organizations gain the ability to directly influence model outputs and behaviors. Unlike closed API-hosted models, which abstract away the data that shapes predictions, a fine-tuned approach enables full transparency and traceability at every step (Kerner, 2025). This data autonomy extends to compliance and governance: fine-tuned models can be validated and audited to meet internal standards or regulatory requirements, such as GDPR or HIPAA, by controlling both the dataset and training pipeline. Enterprises often encounter business-specific language: think of how a bank uses terms like "AML review" or "SOX attestation," or how a retailer encodes SKUs and logistics instructions. HuggingFace Datasets and Tokenizers allow curated ingestion of such language patterns, aligning model vocabulary and context windows with business reality. The result is improved task accuracy and actionable predictions on proprietary workflows.

Operationally, fine-tuned models deliver measurable efficiencies at deployment. Typical fine-tuning cycles, from dataset cleaning to final model packaging with HuggingFace Hub, can be accomplished in weeks, not months, for standardized deployments (AI Fine

Tuned Models Strategy, 2025). Post-processing burdens are sharply reduced because outputs are already adapted to house style, regulatory language, or workflow formatting; for example, custom sentiment analysis models can pre-label escalation cases with consistent terminology, eliminating downstream mapping steps. Processed with company data, these models can support autonomous decisioning, such as auto-triaging customer support tickets or routing compliance alerts, at scale with minimal human intervention. A multinational client saw its SLA breach rate drop by 35% when fine-tuned models replaced generic sentiment tools in front-line ticket triage, reflecting both faster time-to-deployment and reduced manual audit costs. These efficiencies are reinforced by the ability to maintain rapid model updates—fine-tuning supports controlled iterative improvement when new language or processes emerge.

The culmination of these advantages is sustainable market differentiation and increased return on investment. Fine-tuned models become proprietary digital assets: their capabilities cannot be simply purchased or copied by competitors, as they are grounded in the enterprise's unique data and processes (AI Fine Tuned Models Strategy, 2025). In competitive B2B sectors, a logistics firm employing a fine-tuned forecasting model trained on decades of proprietary shipping data can promise more granular, accurate, and reliable delivery ETAs than rivals using off-the-shelf analytics. Comparative studies note that such models can reduce operational delays by 12–20% against baseline predictions. In regulated environments, demonstrable control over AI outputs—achieved through fine-tuning and documented via tools like HuggingFace Model Cards—facilitates both legal defensibility and external certification. The return on investment is realized both in process improvements and in topline growth: organizations capture new clients by demonstrating AI systems precisely adapted to industry needs, and dashboards quantify uplift from improved case resolution rates or reduced compliance exceptions (Kerner, 2025). Ultimately, the strategic deployment of fine-tuned models underpins a scalable platform for innovation, enabling organizations to encode their hardest-won expertise into flexible, defensible digital products.

Project Foundations: Data, Libraries, and Notebooks

Selecting the right dataset is the first critical step when preparing to fine-tune a model with HuggingFace Transformers. Ideal datasets should closely match the downstream task you aim to solve, both in content and structure. Evaluate datasets by checking for clear labels, consistent formatting, data diversity, and size sufficient to avoid overfitting or undertraining. For example, a sentiment classification project should use datasets where each record includes a text and a sentiment label, structured as either JSON objects, CSV rows, or Python dictionaries. HuggingFace datasets like GLUE or IMDb reviews usually follow this pattern, organizing data with fields such as "`text`", "`label`", and sometimes metadata such as "`id`". Avoid datasets with inconsistent labeling, excessive missing information, or poorly sampled data, as these flaws may introduce biases or reduce your model's performance (Schmid, 2020). Always inspect a data sample before proceeding:

```
from datasets import load_dataset

dataset = load_dataset("imdb")
print(dataset["train"][0])
```

Expected output:

```
{'text': "I rented I AM CURIOUS-YELLOW from my video story...",
'label': 0}
```

A quick data glance prevents surprises later in the pipeline and ensures the dataset fits your intended use.

Working efficiently with Jupyter notebooks speeds up iteration and visually organizes your fine-tuning project. Begin by creating a dedicated directory for your project, keeping checkpoints, scripts, and outputs together. Consider using the Jupyter extensions "Table of Contents" for easy navigation, and "Variable Inspector" to monitor memory usage and variable states. Customize notebook settings for better productivity by enabling autocompletion, changing theme, and configuring shortcuts for rapid cell execution. Organize your notebooks into sections: setup, data exploration, preprocessing, training, and results visualization. Each section should contain concise markdown headers and code cells, so you can easily revisit or share your workflow. Always restart the runtime after major library upgrades to prevent dependency conflicts (huggingface, 2020).

Importing the right libraries underpins successful fine-tuning. Make sure your key packages—`transformers`, `datasets`, and `torch`—match the tested versions for your chosen examples. Versioning is essential for compatibility, so install with explicit version numbers:

```
!pip install torch
!pip install "transformers==4.25.1" datasets --upgrade
```

Once installed, import the core libraries and confirm versions:

```
import torch
import transformers
```

```
import datasets

print(torch.__version__)
print(transformers.__version__)
print(datasets.__version__)
```

You should see outputs resembling:

```
1.13.1
4.25.1
2.3.2
```

Initialize HuggingFace components as needed, such as loading a pretrained tokenizer and model scaffold:

```
from transformers import AutoTokenizer,
AutoModelForSequenceClassification

tokenizer = AutoTokenizer.from_pretrained("bert-base-uncased")
model = AutoModelForSequenceClassification.from_pretrained("bert-base-
uncased", num_labels=2)
```

Verifying imports and component initialization at this stage avoids code interruptions later during model training.

Data preprocessing transforms your raw examples into a format suitable for model input. Start by inspecting for duplicate or missing values. Clean text by removing stray whitespace and unwanted symbols with a straightforward function:

```
def clean_text(text):
    return text.strip().replace('\n', ' ')

dataset = dataset.map(lambda x: {"text": clean_text(x["text"])})
```

Proper data splitting ensures unbiased model evaluation. Use HuggingFace split utilities to divide into training, validation, and test sets:

```
split_dataset = dataset["train"].train_test_split(test_size=0.2)
train_ds = split_dataset["train"]
val_ds = split_dataset["test"]

print(f"Train: {len(train_ds)} | Validation: {len(val_ds)}")
```

Expect output such as:

```
Train: 20000 | Validation: 5000
```

Tokenization prepares text for input to transformer networks, aligning with your chosen model from the HuggingFace Hub. Apply batched tokenization and truncate or pad to ensure uniform tensor shapes:

```
def tokenize_function(examples):
    return tokenizer(examples["text"], padding="max_length",
truncation=True, max_length=128)
```

```
tokenized_datasets = train_ds.map(tokenize_function, batched=True)
```

Reviewing a processed entry helps confirm preparation is complete:

```
print(tokenized_datasets[0].keys())  # Output: dict_keys(['text',
'label', 'input_ids', 'attention_mask'])
```

This sequence of foundational steps builds a consistent environment, enabling seamless transition into model configuration and iterative training. Attention to these details sets up efficient hands-on development and minimizes technical interruptions as you proceed to deeper fine-tuning phases (Schmid, 2020; huggingface, 2020).

Step-by-Step Fine-Tuning with HuggingFace

Choosing the right pretrained model is the first decision when starting fine-tuning. For a customer-focused text classification task, consider instruction-tuned models like meta-llama/Llama-3-8b-instruct for a balance of speed and accuracy, or smaller models if resources are limited (Rao, 2025). Begin by defining the base model and loading its weights and tokenizer:

```
from transformers import AutoModelForSequenceClassification,
AutoTokenizer

model_name = "distilbert-base-uncased"  # Swap for models like "meta-
llama/Llama-3-8b-instruct" as needed
```

```
tokenizer = AutoTokenizer.from_pretrained(model_name)
model = AutoModelForSequenceClassification.from_pretrained(model_name,
num_labels=2)
```

Expected output:

```
Downloading: distilbert-base-uncased... Some weights of the model were
not initialized.
```

Here, you load both architecture weights and tokenizer. Specify num_labels for your classification problem. Swap model names to match your task and hardware, referencing Hugging Face's model hub as needed (Resources for Using Hugging Face with Amazon SageMaker AI - Amazon SageMaker AI, 2025).

Setting hyperparameters affects model convergence and resource usage. Key parameters include learning_rate, per_device_train_batch_size, num_train_epochs, and weight_decay. Carefully tune learning_rate—too high can destabilize training; too low leads to slow learning:

```
from transformers import TrainingArguments

training_args = TrainingArguments(
    output_dir='./results',
    evaluation_strategy="steps",
    save_steps=500,
    learning_rate=2e-5,
    per_device_train_batch_size=16,
    per_device_eval_batch_size=32,
```

```
    num_train_epochs=3,
    weight_decay=0.01,
    logging_dir='./logs',
    logging_steps=100
)
```

Estimate GPU memory requirements by multiplying batch_size by model size. Use gradient checkpointing to save memory with larger models (Rao, 2025).

To tokenize a CSV dataset containing customer support texts and labels:

```
from datasets import load_dataset

raw_datasets = load_dataset('csv', data_files={'train': 'train.csv',
'test': 'test.csv'})

def preprocess_function(examples):
    return tokenizer(examples['text'], truncation=True,
padding='max_length', max_length=128)

tokenized_datasets = raw_datasets.map(preprocess_function,
batched=True)
```

Watch for tokenization mismatches; ensure max_length is reasonable for your domain. The map function batches the transformation for efficiency.

To set up the trainer with early stopping and checkpointing:

```
from transformers import Trainer, EarlyStoppingCallback

trainer = Trainer(
    model=model,
    args=training_args,
    train_dataset=tokenized_datasets['train'],
    eval_dataset=tokenized_datasets['test'],
    callbacks=[EarlyStoppingCallback(early_stopping_patience=3)]
)
```

Resume training from checkpoints if needed, and always set random seeds for reproducibility.

For real-time monitoring and reproducible logs, integrate MLflow:

```
import mlflow
from transformers.integrations import MLflowCallback

mlflow.set_tracking_uri('file:./mlruns/')
mlflow.set_experiment('text-classification')
trainer.add_callback(MLflowCallback(mlflow))
```

Once training starts, MLflow shows learning curves and logs artifacts. Weights & Biases or TensorBoard are alternatives depending on infrastructure.

After training, save the model and tokenizer:

```
trainer.save_model('./exported-model')
tokenizer.save_pretrained('./exported-model')
```

Always export the tokenizer; mismatched tokenizers frequently cause inference failures. Reload for inference:

```
from transformers import pipeline, AutoModelForSequenceClassification,
AutoTokenizer

inference_model =
AutoModelForSequenceClassification.from_pretrained('./exported-model')
inference_tokenizer = AutoTokenizer.from_pretrained('./exported-
model')

classifier = pipeline("text-classification", model=inference_model,
tokenizer=inference_tokenizer)
```

Expected output for an input:

```
[{'label': 'LABEL_0', 'score': 0.987}]
```

Validate compatibility between model and tokenizer to avoid silent failures.

Saving training arguments and metadata enhances reproducibility. Use checkpoint directories to store weights and configs, and integrate with cloud storage or SageMaker registries for distribution (Resources for Using Hugging Face with Amazon SageMaker AI - Amazon SageMaker AI, 2025).

Finally, evaluate performance on held-out sets with appropriate metrics, and consider cross-validation strategies to ensure robustness in production deployments.

Validating and Improving Your Model

Evaluation Metrics for Model Assessment

Assessing your model's effectiveness begins with the right evaluation metrics. In classification, accuracy, precision, recall, and F1 score are fundamental. Accuracy is the proportion of correct predictions over all predictions and is easy to interpret but can mask poor performance on imbalanced datasets. Consider a spam detector: if only 5% of emails are spam, a model predicting all emails as non-spam will have 95% accuracy but be useless. Precision measures how many selected items are relevant. In a medical diagnosis, high precision ensures few false positives. Recall highlights the proportion of true positives found out of all actual positive examples, which is critical in safety-critical applications—like identifying all patients with a disease. F1 score balances precision and recall, useful when you need a single measure that penalizes extreme values in either metric (Srivastava, 2019).

With HuggingFace's datasets and evaluate libraries, it's straightforward to calculate these metrics. Suppose you have model outputs preds and ground-truth labels labels:

```
from evaluate import load

accuracy = load("accuracy")
precision = load("precision")
recall = load("recall")
f1 = load("f1")
```

```
acc = accuracy.compute(predictions=preds, references=labels)
prec = precision.compute(predictions=preds, references=labels)
rec = recall.compute(predictions=preds, references=labels)
f1_score = f1.compute(predictions=preds, references=labels)
```

Choose metrics that match your context. Use accuracy for balanced multiclass problems, precision in domains prioritizing false positive reduction, recall when catching every positive is vital, and F1 when you need balance.

Cross-Validation Techniques

Reliable validation goes beyond simple splits. Cross-validation ensures the trained model generalizes to unseen data by rotating through training and test partitions. In k-fold cross-validation, you split data into k equal subsets. For each round, one subset becomes the validation set while the rest are for training, cycling through all folds. This ensures every data point is tested exactly once and trains the optimizer on the entire dataset over repeated runs, reducing bias and variance compared to a single held-out sample (GeeksforGeeks, 2017).

For example, with 5-fold cross-validation, the dataset splits into five parts. The model first trains on four and tests on the fifth; this repeats, shifting the fold used for validation. The reported metric is the average performance across all folds. A numerical illustration: in a 1000-sample dataset with 5 folds, each fold is 200 instances. Each model gets 800 for training, 200 for testing, cycling through the entire data.

Implementing k-fold on HuggingFace datasets looks like:

```python
from datasets import load_dataset
import numpy as np

dataset = load_dataset('your_dataset')
n_folds = 5
indices = np.arange(len(dataset['train']))
fold_size = len(indices) // n_folds
folds = [indices[i*fold_size:(i+1)*fold_size] for i in range(n_folds)]
results = []

for fold in range(n_folds):
    val_idx = folds[fold]
    train_idx = np.hstack([folds[i] for i in range(n_folds) if i != fold])

    train_subset = dataset['train'].select(train_idx.tolist())
    val_subset = dataset['train'].select(val_idx.tolist())

    # Initialize model and training here ...
    # Append evaluation metrics on val_subset to results

# Compute average score across folds
```

Interpret cross-validation by examining not just mean performance, but also stability (standard deviation) across folds, helping reveal overfitting or unstable learning (Srivastava, 2019; GeeksforGeeks, 2017).

Error Analysis Methods

After calculating metrics, probing the "why" behind prediction errors leads to powerful improvements. Start by collecting misclassified examples. For instance, filter where preds ≠ labels. Next, categorize errors—do false positives cluster around certain rare classes, or does the model underperform on specific input lengths or topics?

```
import pandas as pd

df = pd.DataFrame({'pred': preds, 'label': labels, 'input': input_texts})
errors = df[df['pred'] != df['label']]
```

Spotting repetitive misclassification patterns exposes systematic problems, like poor handling of ambiguous language, class imbalances, or outliers. For NLP, leveraging huggingface_hub visualization tools can surface patterns (e.g., via confusion matrices or heatmaps) grouped by label or input features. Tackling issues like these by augmenting data, rebalancing classes, or refining preprocessing often corrects entire categories of errors.

Iterative Model Improvement

Improving model performance is an ongoing, data-driven process. Start with an initial baseline, record all current scores and error categories. Based on observed failure patterns, prioritize fixes: maybe hyperparameter tuning, feature engineering, or more data curation.

Set up a version-controlled workflow—after every change (new loss parameters, new data augmentation, etc.), rerun your evaluation pipeline and log results. For hyperparameters, tools like HuggingFace Optuna integration support automated sweeps:

```
from transformers import TrainingArguments, Trainer

training_args = TrainingArguments(...)
model = ... # Initialize model
trainer = Trainer(model=model, args=training_args, train_dataset=...,
eval_dataset=...)

# Use Trainer.hyperparameter_search for tuning
```

By comparing before-and-after results on the same validation/data splits, you'll see if the changes move the needle (GeeksforGeeks, 2017; Srivastava, 2019). This record also makes final documentation and sharing transparent, so collaborators understand how and why model decisions were made and can build reliably on your improvements.

Documenting and Sharing Fine-Tuning Results

A well-documented, easy-to-explore AI model not only showcases the hard work put into fine-tuning but also encourages responsible adoption in the community. Model cards are the backbone of this process, providing detailed insight into model structure, intended use, performance, and potential limitations. A complete Hugging Face model card should start with concise model details: include the architecture (for example, "BERT base, uncased, 12-layer transformer"), the release date, version, and license type. Responsible parties and contact information help others know where to turn for questions or contributions.

Performance metrics are central—state them clearly and specify the context.

For instance, *"This model reached an F1-score of 0.89 on the IMDB test set for sentiment classification, using the provided evaluation script."*

Describe the sources of training data with as much granularity as possible such as, *"Trained on 100,000 IMDb movie reviews balanced across positive and negative sentiment."*

Include any preprocessing steps that impact reproducibility or fairness. Don't forget to flag known limitations:

"Accuracy drops by 8% on reviews less than 20 words in length or containing non-English text."

Such candor helps future adopters use the model with the right expectations.

Usage guidelines keep users on the right track. Write clear instructions:

"To use this model with Transformers library, run: model = AutoModelForSequenceClassification.from_pretrained('username/finetuned-bert-imdb')".

Offer caveats about scope:

"Not intended for product review sentiment outside movie domain."

In the ethical considerations section, acknowledge risks—for example, *"Potential for bias toward popular film genres; mitigation steps included stratified sampling and subgroup evaluation"* (Bhat et al., 2023).

A strong model card is organized, specific, and written for a broad technical audience. Use plain language, bullet points, and code snippets for clarity. Compare *"Training Data: 80% MovieLens, 20% Rotten Tomatoes, shuffled and tokenized"* to a vague "Trained on various datasets."

When presenting metrics, mention how you calculated them: "*Precision calculated per IMDb guidelines, full script provided below.*"

Transparency here prevents confusion and builds trust (Bhat et al., 2023).

A professional code repository backs up the model with everything required for others to reproduce, adapt, or extend the work. Start with a clear folder structure such as:

```
/model
    /src
        train.py
        eval.py
    /config
        config.yaml
    /data
        README.md
    /notebooks
        example_finetuning.ipynb
requirements.txt
```

```
README.md
LICENSE
```

`README.md` should summarize the model, cite datasets, and explain installation and usage succinctly. For example,

"Clone this repo, install dependencies from requirements.txt, and run `python src/train.py --config config/config.yaml`."

Include exact package versions to prevent mismatch problems. License files clarify usage rights, while a dedicated section or file about data privacy signals respect for end-user data: *"All training data was publicly available. No user-identifiable data was stored"* (Bhat et al., 2023).

Offer sample output—*"After setup, expect test accuracy near 88%"*—and surface potential issues with environment or hardware, like required GPU size. List optional scripts or Jupyter Notebooks for easier exploration.

Performance visualizations turn technical achievements into digestible insights. Start with fundamentals like confusion matrices for classification tasks, produced using libraries such as scikit-learn's `plot_confusion_matrix`. ROC curves are invaluable for highlighting a model's ability to rank positive and negative examples—show thresholds with color coding or annotations for clarity.

Plotting the training and validation loss over epochs paints a vivid picture of convergence and potential overfitting. A simple matplotlib code example:

```
plt.plot(history['train_loss'], label='Train Loss')
plt.plot(history['val_loss'], label='Validation Loss')
plt.xlabel('Epoch')
plt.ylabel('Loss')
plt.legend()
plt.show()
```

Benchmark tables or bar charts comparing your model to baselines reinforce credibility. Highlight strengths with annotations, e.g., *"Model outperforms baseline by 3 F1 points on minority class."* Use consistent color palettes and focus on legibility over excessive styling.

AI communities help amplify your model's reach. Hugging Face Hub, GitHub, Reddit's r/MachineLearning, and AI-oriented Discord servers let you share, gather feedback, and collaborate. In your posts, provide a summary, code links, a motivation statement, and explicit requests: *"Seeking feedback on generalizability; does the model lose performance on non-English data?"* Encourage suggestions through issue trackers or dedicated discussion threads.

Respond to input with gratitude and actionable follow-ups—*"Thanks for the bug report! Added a patch to address tokenizer mismatch."* Document significant user-driven updates in a `CHANGELOG.md` file. Periodically update the model card with new metrics, user-reported limitations, or mitigations. These steps show commitment, foster trust, and make the project a living resource for the AI community (Bhat et al., 2023).

Bringing It All Together

Now that we have explored the full process of fine-tuning AI models with HuggingFace tools—from preparing data and setting up environments to training, validating, and documenting custom models—you are equipped to build targeted solutions that meet real-world needs. This foundation enables you to create AI systems that handle specialized language, improve accuracy on critical tasks, and maintain control over data and compliance. With these skills, you can confidently move forward to experiment with more complex models, integrate monitoring and deployment workflows, and contribute valuable, well-documented AI assets to your projects or teams. Embracing this hands-on approach lays a strong groundwork for developing effective, transparent, and scalable AI applications ready to solve industry challenges.

Chapter 6
From Notebook to Web App: Deploying AI with FastAPI and Docker

Deploying a model is where the work truly begins," my mentor once told me as we stared at rows of code in a Jupyter notebook. At first, I didn't understand. The model ran perfectly in isolation—why did it matter if it wasn't live and accessible to users? But over time I learned that turning a prototype into a functioning web application is what separates theoretical projects from solutions that make real impact. It's the step that shows you can not only build an algorithm but also engineer reliable, scalable systems that solve actual problems under unpredictable conditions.

Deployment reveals challenges no notebook ever exposes: handling messy inputs, managing scaling demands, monitoring performance, and keeping systems secure and available. For aspiring AI engineers and developers transitioning into this field, mastering deployment is essential because it bridges the gap between experimentation and production-ready software.

This chapter takes you through that critical journey—from wrapping your AI model inside a FastAPI service, containerizing it with Docker, launching it on cloud platforms, to presenting your project effectively. Understanding these processes will equip you with practical skills that employers value, enabling you to move beyond isolated code toward delivering AI-powered applications that meet real user needs and thrive in dynamic environments.

Why Deployment Is the Deciding Factor in AI Careers

Unlocking real value from artificial intelligence projects requires more than just building models in isolation. For AI engineers, the true differentiator is the ability to turn prototypes into deployed web applications that operate reliably for real users. In today's AI-driven job market, having deployed applications makes a candidate highly attractive. Recruiters and industry leaders consistently state that deployed projects stand out because they reveal far more than skill at constructing models—they demonstrate the engineering discipline required to solve authentic business problems.

For example, a prototype language model housed only in a Jupyter notebook demonstrates technical curiosity, but when that same model is delivered as a production API using FastAPI or served through a robust Docker container, it becomes an operational business asset. Many companies now expect engineers to show evidence of project deployment; recent surveys highlight that nearly 70% of AI job listings require experience with taking ML solutions live or building APIs for model serving (Salerno, 2024; 10 Software Engineering Skills Needed to Lead in the AI Economy - the Quantic Blog, 2025). The difference can mean landing an interview or fading into the noise among thousands of notebook portfolios.

Once a model is deployed and available outside the lab, its immediate impact on end users becomes clear. Deployed AI systems address real needs—matching customers with products, personalizing recommendations, flagging harmful content, or automating document workflows. When people interact with these applications, you can measure value with metrics like response time, uptime, and satisfaction ratings. Feedback loops are essential: Gmail's spam filter, refined through millions of user interactions, proves how real-world usage drives continuous model improvement. In contrast, notebook-bound projects remain invisible—unseen by stakeholders, untested in actual use, and unable to deliver lasting impact. Top AI companies like OpenAI and Google stress that iterating on real products exposed to real users is key to long-term success. Deployment is the only way to learn from actual performance, refine functionality, and deliver tangible improvements (Salerno, 2024).

Reliability is the next defining factor. In development, models see sanitized, controlled data. But real-world usage introduces messy, unpredictable scenarios. A FastAPI backend must cope with network issues, malformed inputs, usage spikes, and data patterns unseen during training. For example, a fraud detection system might perform well in tests but face evolving strategies, inconsistent formats, and transaction floods in production. Surviving this shift—from lab data to production traffic—earns a model its place in a real tech stack. Engineers who manage unexpected requests, software updates, system failures, and model drift prove they can deliver robust solutions. Building health checks, dashboards, alerts, and fallback strategies is what defines high-impact software teams today (Salerno, 2024; *10 Software Engineering Skills Needed to Lead in the AI Economy* – Quantic Blog, 2025).

Speed of innovation is where deployment truly sets high performers apart. Practices like containerization with Docker and CI/CD pipelines (e.g., GitHub Actions, Jenkins) allow rapid rollout of new features, bug fixes, and model updates. The cycle—develop, deploy, observe, improve—shrinks from weeks to hours. A recommendation engine released via FastAPI can be updated in real time based on engagement metrics, allowing sharp responsiveness to user needs or trends. In competitive markets, the ability to adapt quickly determines who leads. AI-native deployment pipelines are enabling teams to outpace traditional cycles by continuously iterating on both models and their intcgrations (Quantic Blog, 2025).

Engineers who master deployment gain a full-stack perspective: they bridge concept to product, ensure stability, adapt to change, and deliver continuous innovation. This skill set distinguishes high-performing AI engineers and lays the foundation for tackling scalable, complex AI systems. Deployment isn't just a final step—it's the proving ground for applied excellence (Salerno, 2024; Quantic Blog, 2025).

Building a Production-Ready API: Coding Tutorial with FastAPI

When converting an AI model from an experiment in a Jupyter notebook into a production-grade service, FastAPI offers an efficient, robust path. The foundation begins with defining endpoints that expose your model as a REST API. Start by importing FastAPI, creating an app instance, and implementing simple GET and POST paths. For example, suppose you have a trained spam classifier loaded as model. The basic app structure could look like this:

```
from fastapi import FastAPI, HTTPException
from pydantic import BaseModel

app = FastAPI()

# Placeholder for your already-trained AI model
def predict_spam(text: str) -> bool:
    # Imagine this function runs your model
    return "spam" in text

class Message(BaseModel):
    text: str
```

```python
@app.post("/predict")
def predict(message: Message):
    result = predict_spam(message.text)
    return {"spam": result}
```

In this setup, sending a POST request to `/predict` with JSON like `{ "text": "Buy now" }` would return `{ "spam": true }`. This method adheres to REST conventions, cleanly separates model input from result, and provides status code `200` on success. To increase reliability, add error handling for malformed data and model inference exceptions, returning descriptive errors with appropriate status codes.

For robust input validation, Pydantic schemas play a central role. Defining input models as subclasses of `BaseModel` ensures strict type and structure validation, which blocks many common bugs early. FastAPI automatically enforces constraints and recognizes optional or required fields. For a regression model serving multiple features, the schema might grow:

```python
class Features(BaseModel):
    age: int
    income: float
    occupation: str

@app.post("/predict-income")
def predict_income(features: Features):
    # replace with real model prediction
```

```
    prediction = 50000 + features.age * 100 - features.income * 0.05
    return {"predicted_income": prediction}
```

Requests missing fields, submitting improper types, or malformed JSON trigger an HTTP 422 response with clear details. Custom data validation can be implemented using Pydantic's validators for domain-specific checks. Validating user input at the schema level aids data integrity, limiting inference errors due to dirty inputs and simplifying client-side troubleshooting (First Steps - FastAPI, n.d.).

AI deployments must handle heavy concurrent traffic as models scale to real-world production. FastAPI intrinsically supports asynchronous endpoints using Python's `async def` syntax, which enables the app to process many requests simultaneously without blocking threads—a key factor for serving high-throughput inference. Adapting our earlier POST path for async inference:

```
from fastapi import BackgroundTasks

@app.post("/predict-async")
async def predict_async(message: Message):
    # Assume async_model_predict is an async call to your AI model
    result = await async_model_predict(message.text)
    return {"spam": result}
```

This asynchronous approach is indispensable if your model inference leverages slow I/O, long-running computations, or you're orchestrating multiple remote services (FastAPI, 2023). To ensure maximum efficiency, avoid blocking operations inside `async` functions—use only non-blocking libraries for database or network access in async routes. Bottlenecks from synchronous code will reduce FastAPI's performance gains. Evaluate your model's serving logic for true async compatibility and test at scale with real-world loads.

FastAPI automatically provides interactive API documentation, tightly integrated with the OpenAPI specification. As soon as a route is defined, it appears in the built-in Swagger UI at `/docs` and the alternative ReDoc at /redoc. Each route is documented with its HTTP method, parameters, request and response bodies, types, and example payloads. This immediate feedback accelerates development, making it easy for teams and clients to understand and test endpoints without additional documentation work. Testing a POST endpoint for model inference can be done directly in the browser, reducing integration bugs and streamlining collaboration across backend, frontend, and product teams (First Steps - FastAPI, n.d.; FastAPI, 2023).

As you build a complete API for your AI solution, follow a structure with clear separation for model loading, endpoint definitions, and reusable utility code. Establish versioned API prefixes (`/v1/predict`, `/v2/predict`) to handle model upgrades without breaking existing integrations. Implement comprehensive error handlers for predictable responses, logging inference errors, and tracking abnormal inputs for monitoring performance and data drift.

These best practices ensure that your FastAPI application provides stable, scalable model inference endpoints. This RESTful service can then be containerized for resilient, reproducible deployment as the next step—paving the way to serve powerful AI models at scale with confidence (FastAPI, 2023).

Dockerizing Your AI App: Step-by-Step Guide to Containerization

Hands-On Dockerization for AI API Applications

Containerizing a FastAPI-based AI application begins with a well-crafted Dockerfile. Starting from a slim official Python image ensures a secure and lightweight foundation. Multi-stage builds help keep the resulting image minimal and efficient, especially when managing large AI frameworks and dependencies. Here's a typical Dockerfile for a FastAPI AI service, including model loading and inference:

```
# Stage 1: Build
FROM python:3.11-slim as builder
WORKDIR /app

# Install build dependencies
RUN apt-get update && apt-get install -y --no-install-recommends gcc

# Install Python dependencies
COPY requirements.txt .
RUN pip install --user --upgrade pip && \
    pip install --user -r requirements.txt

# Stage 2: Runtime
FROM python:3.11-slim
WORKDIR /app

# Copy dependencies from the builder
COPY --from=builder /root/.local /root/.local
```

```
# Copy application files
COPY . .

# Set environment variables
ENV MODEL_PATH=/models/model.pt
ENV PYTHONPATH=/app

# Add model volume mount point
VOLUME ["/models"]

# Expose FastAPI port
EXPOSE 8000

# Launch the app using Uvicorn
CMD ["sh", "-c", "PATH=$PATH:/root/.local/bin exec uvicorn main:app --host 0.0.0.0 --port 8000"]
```

Key Notes: - The builder stage installs dependencies, keeping runtime images lean. - `requirements.txt` must list FastAPI, Uvicorn, and AI libraries like `PyTorch` or `TensorFlow`. - `VOLUME ["/models"]` allows model updates without rebuilding the image.

To build your Docker image:

```
docker build -t fastapi-ai-app:latest .
```

Successful output should include lines like:

```
Successfully built 12345abcdef
Successfully tagged fastapi-ai-app:latest
```

If errors occur (e.g., missing dependencies), check your requirements.txt:

```
ERROR: Could not find a version that satisfies the requirement
xyz==x.y.z
```

Running and Testing the FastAPI Container

To launch your container and mount your model file:

```
docker run -p 8000:8000 -v $(pwd)/models:/models -e
MODEL_PATH=/models/model.pt fastapi-ai-app:latest
```

- `-p 8000:8000` exposes the container port.
- `-v $(pwd)/models:/models` mounts your local `models/` folder.
- `-e MODEL_PATH=...` allows flexible runtime config.

Missing models will trigger errors like:

```
FileNotFoundError: [Errno 2] No such file or directory:
'/models/model.pt'
```

Ensure your file exists in the correct path.

Container Networking for Model Serving

To allow service-to-service communication:

```
docker network create ai-app-network
```

```
docker run --network ai-app-network -p 8000:8000 -v
$(pwd)/models:/models fastapi-ai-app:latest
```

Use named networks to connect your API with databases, monitoring tools, or other containers.

Using Docker Compose for Multi-Service Management

Here's a sample `docker-compose.yml` for a FastAPI app with Redis:

```yaml
version: '3.8'
services:
  api:
    image: fastapi-ai-app:latest
    build: .
    ports:
      - "8000:8000"
    environment:
      - MODEL_PATH=/models/model.pt
    volumes:
      - ./models:/models
    networks:
      - ai-app-network

  redis:
    image: redis:7 alpine
    networks:
      - ai-app-network
```

```
networks:
  ai-app-network:
    driver: bridge
```

Launch all services with:

```
docker compose up --build
```

If services can't resolve each other, confirm they share the same network.

Best Practices for AI Containers

Use slim base images or GPU-optimized ones (e.g., CUDA-enabled). - Keep credentials out of image layers—use environment variables. - Leverage multi-stage builds for clean images. - Mount large models via volumes. - Restrict network access and exposed ports.

With your FastAPI AI app containerized, you're ready for the next phase: deploying to the cloud and scaling access to your model-based services (GeeksforGeeks, 2019; Baker, 2023).

Deploying to the Cloud: Local Testing and Public Launch

Before releasing your FastAPI-based AI application to the public, thorough local testing is essential to ensure reliability and fault tolerance. Begin by verifying that your

Dockerized FastAPI app behaves as expected with both unit and integration tests. For example, using `pytest`, create a test file such as

`test_main.py`:

```
import requests


def test_predict():
    url = "http://localhost:8000/predict"
    sample_input = {"text": "hello world"}
    response = requests.post(url, json=sample_input)
    assert response.status_code == 200
    assert "prediction" in response.json()
```

To test the app locally:

```
docker build -t myfastapiapp .
docker run -p 8000:8000 myfastapiapp
```

If the container starts successfully, you'll see logs like:

```
INFO:     Started server process [1]
INFO:     Application startup complete.
INFO:     Uvicorn running on http://0.0.0.0:8000
```

Configure Python logging to aid debugging:

```
import logging


logging.basicConfig(
```

```
    level=logging.INFO,
    format='%(asctime)s %(levelname)s %(message)s',
    handlers=[
        logging.StreamHandler()
    ]
)

logger = logging.getLogger(__name__)
logger.info("Starting FastAPI application")
```

Use consistent log formatting and levels across development and production.

Load Testing with Locust

To assess performance and scalability, install Locust and define a basic load test:

```
from locust import HttpUser, task


class FastApiUser(HttpUser):
    @task
    def predict(self):
        self.client.post("/predict", json={"text": "load test"})
```

Run the test with:

```
locust -f locustfile.py --host=http://localhost:8000
```

Monitor response times and errors in Locust's web UI. Test for common input variations and edge cases to uncover performance bottlenecks.

Use try-except blocks to handle inference errors without exposing internal details:

```
from fastapi import HTTPException


@app.post("/predict")
async def predict_endpoint(data: InputDataModel):
    try:
        prediction = model.predict(data.text)
        return {"prediction": prediction}
    except Exception as e:
        logger.error(f"Prediction error: {e}")
        raise HTTPException(status_code=500, detail="Prediction
failed.")
```

Pushing to the Cloud

Once testing is complete, push your Docker image to a registry like Docker Hub or Amazon ECR:

```
docker tag myfastapiapp mydockerusername/myfastapiapp:latest
docker push mydockerusername/myfastapiapp:latest
```

For AWS Elastic Beanstalk, create a `Dockerrun.aws.json`:

```
{
  "AWSEBDockerrunVersion": 2,
  "containerDefinitions": [
```

```
    {
      "name": "fastapi_app",
      "image": "mydockerusername/myfastapiapp:latest",
      "essential": true,
      "portMappings": [{
        "containerPort": 8000,
        "hostPort": 8000
      }],
      "environment": [
        {"name": "API_KEY", "value": "secure-api-key-value"}
      ]
    }
  ]
}
```

Then run:

```
eb init -p docker fastapi-app
eb create fastapi-app-env
eb open fastapi-app-env
```

Deploying on Heroku

```
heroku container:login
heroku create fastapi-heroku-app
heroku container:push web -a fastapi-heroku-app
heroku container:release web -a fastapi-heroku-app
heroku config:set API_KEY=secure-api-key-value
```

Health Checks

Use a lightweight endpoint for readiness probes:

```
@app.get("/health")
def health():
    return {"status": "ok"}
```

Check deployment status with:

```
curl https://fastapi-heroku-app.herokuapp.com/health
```

A healthy response returns:

```
{"status": "ok"}
```

Security Considerations

Avoid hardcoding secrets. Use environment variables and secure secret managers instead. Keep .env out of version control:

```
API_KEY=secure-api-key
```

```
import os
api_key = os.getenv("API_KEY")
```

API Key Authentication

```
from fastapi import Depends, Header, HTTPException


def verify_api_key(x_api_key: str = Header(...)):
    if x_api_key != os.environ["API_KEY"]:
        raise HTTPException(status_code=401, detail="Unauthorized")


@app.post("/predict")
async def predict(data: InputDataModel, api_key: str =
Depends(verify_api_key)):
    # ...
```

Add rate limiting with middleware such as slowapi, and restrict endpoint exposure. Rotate keys regularly and audit logs for suspicious behavior.

Enforce least-privilege access through IAM settings. Use API usage quotas and alerts to protect from overuse or leaks.

With Docker, FastAPI, and secure deployment practices, your AI app is ready to scale safely from local development to global users.

Presenting and Sharing Your Deployed Project

Effectively showcasing your deployed AI application is critical for demonstrating its value, gaining stakeholder support, and collecting meaningful feedback. Combining live demos, video walkthroughs, clear documentation, and integrated feedback systems creates a well-rounded presentation strategy that increases adoption and drives iterative improvement.

Live Demos

A well-executed live demo connects directly with your audience, showcasing core features and use cases in real time. Start by preparing a detailed script that outlines key user tasks and highlights moments where the AI system excels. Include paths for realistic use cases, expected outputs, edge cases, and graceful error handling.

To ensure reliability:

- Run backup instances on secondary servers.
- Keep offline versions of models and data ready.
- Set up fallback routes in your frontend.

Enhance the experience with:

- UI focus highlights (via CSS overlays).
- Automation tools like Selenium or Playwright to simulate steps.
- Verbose logging to reveal reasoning or decisions made by the model.

Minimize latency by preloading data and using screen mirroring or large displays for group settings. Avoid showcasing unstable or unreleased features. Evaluate the demo's success through user engagement, script completion rates, and feedback surveys.

Video Walkthroughs

Video walkthroughs enable asynchronous sharing of your project with reviewers, recruiters, or collaborators. Record in 1080p or higher using tools like OBS Studio or Camtasia. Ensure that text, UI components, and model outputs are clearly visible with good contrast and legibility.

Tips for professional-quality results:

- Use a unidirectional condenser microphone at 48kHz.
- Write a concise, aligned voiceover script.
- Edit out delays and distractions.
- Add callouts, fast-forwards, and chapters for clarity.

Use platforms like YouTube to host your video and monitor retention, engagement, and link clicks. Always rehearse the full walkthrough to avoid interruptions.

Documentation

Thorough documentation is essential for usability and credibility. Your `README.md` should include:

- A project summary.
- Setup instructions (with exact commands).

- Usage examples.
- Troubleshooting and FAQs.

For production systems, add:

- Architecture diagrams.
- Backup and failover strategies.
- Security practices.
- Links to model cards and audit logs.

Example API call:

```
POST /api/predict
{
  "input": "Sample prompt for inference"
}
```

Keep dependencies up to date and document all changes. Measure effectiveness by support ticket reduction and successful user onboarding.

Feedback Systems

Incorporate user feedback channels directly into your application. Use tools like Formik (for React) or integrate third-party platforms such as Hotjar, Qualtrics, or Discord. Categorize and tag incoming feedback for triage using APIs, then route insights to project management platforms like Jira or Planview.

Build a feedback loop:

- Regularly review input in team meetings.
- Document improvements in versioned release notes.
- Track feedback response times and implementation rates.

Avoid ignoring user feedback or leaving it untracked. Use dashboards to monitor trends and ensure users feel heard.

By applying these best practices, you elevate the quality and professionalism of your AI application's presentation—demonstrating technical maturity, improving user experience, and strengthening your presence in the broader AI ecosystem.

Chapter 7
Smart Monitoring: Tracking, Logging, and Improving with MLflow

Imagine deploying an AI model that excels in the lab—only to see its performance drop in the real world. Accuracy dips, predictions become erratic, and no one knows why. This is where monitoring becomes mission-critical. Behind every successful AI system is a layer of constant observation—spotting issues early, identifying trends, and guiding iterative improvements. Without it, models turn into black boxes, silently failing and eroding user trust.

This chapter introduces monitoring as a vital component of the AI lifecycle and presents **MLflow** as a practical tool for tracking, logging, and visualization. You'll learn how to integrate MLflow into your workflows, capture key parameters and metrics, and analyze your results for insight and improvement. We'll also explore how to translate monitoring insights into better models and resilient pipelines that support continuous development and operational success.

Why Monitoring Matters: Building Trust and Driving Progress

Professional-grade AI systems distinguish themselves through robust monitoring. It's not just about error detection—it's about accountability, insight, and trust. Monitoring supports four key objectives:

- **Early failure detection**
- **Operational transparency**
- **Data-driven improvement**
- **Stakeholder confidence**

Early Failure Detection

AI systems function in complex, unpredictable environments. Minor issues can escalate quickly—unless caught in time. Monitoring frameworks are your early warning system. Take manufacturing: telemetry sensors on factory robots can detect deviations in vibration patterns, flagging potential mechanical failures before they cause downtime (Anglen, 2024). Critical metrics to track include:

- Inference latency
- Memory usage spikes
- Prediction anomalies
- Hardware temperature thresholds

For example, a logistics platform using AI to predict equipment failures can monitor error rates and sensor data. If thresholds are exceeded, automated alerts via Slack or email trigger real-time responses—pausing deployments or switching to backups. These proactive measures reduce downtime, cut costs, and shield business operations (Anglen, 2024).

Operational Transparency

Regulations and internal governance demand that AI decisions be explainable and traceable. That means keeping detailed logs:

- Timestamps of model execution
- Input/output data snapshots
- Model version identifiers
- Parameter changes and manual overrides

Centralized logs speed up troubleshooting. Say a financial model misflags a transaction. With traceable logs, teams can instantly review inputs, the model version used, and the environment context—accelerating diagnosis and resolution (Adelakun, 2022).

This level of auditability fosters reliability, especially in high-stakes sectors like finance or healthcare. Clear documentation of every step ensures your system can be trusted and verified.

Data-Driven Improvement

Real-time performance metrics help teams spot where models struggle—and where they shine. Track:

- Precision, recall, and F1 score
- Drift statistics
- Inference latency trends

For example, if a fraud detection model shows increased false positives during high transaction volumes, you might need to redesign features or retrain with newer data (Adelakun, 2022).

Monitoring uncovers hidden inefficiencies. Patterns in logged errors might reveal mislabeled training data or poor generalization. With historical logs, teams can compare past experiments, roll back bad deployments, or even automate tuning jobs based on prior performance (Anglen, 2024).

Use cases include tracking:

- Feature importance post-deployment
- Behavior under new data streams
- User feedback metrics

This systematic approach drives objective, measurable improvements across your AI pipeline.

Stakeholder Trust

Monitoring builds confidence—not just among engineers, but across business and leadership teams. Dashboards, compliance logs, and alert summaries help executives assess model performance without diving into technical minutiae.

High-level metrics to report:

- Uptime
- Accuracy trends
- Data throughput
- Incident and exception rates

Custom alerts for threshold breaches keep leadership informed and engaged. Consistent reporting fosters credibility and shows that your team is proactive, not reactive. Transparent discussions around detected issues and resolutions help reduce resistance to AI adoption (Adelakun, 2022).

As regulations tighten, demonstrating responsible AI usage becomes essential. Monitoring isn't just about compliance—it's a signal of professionalism.

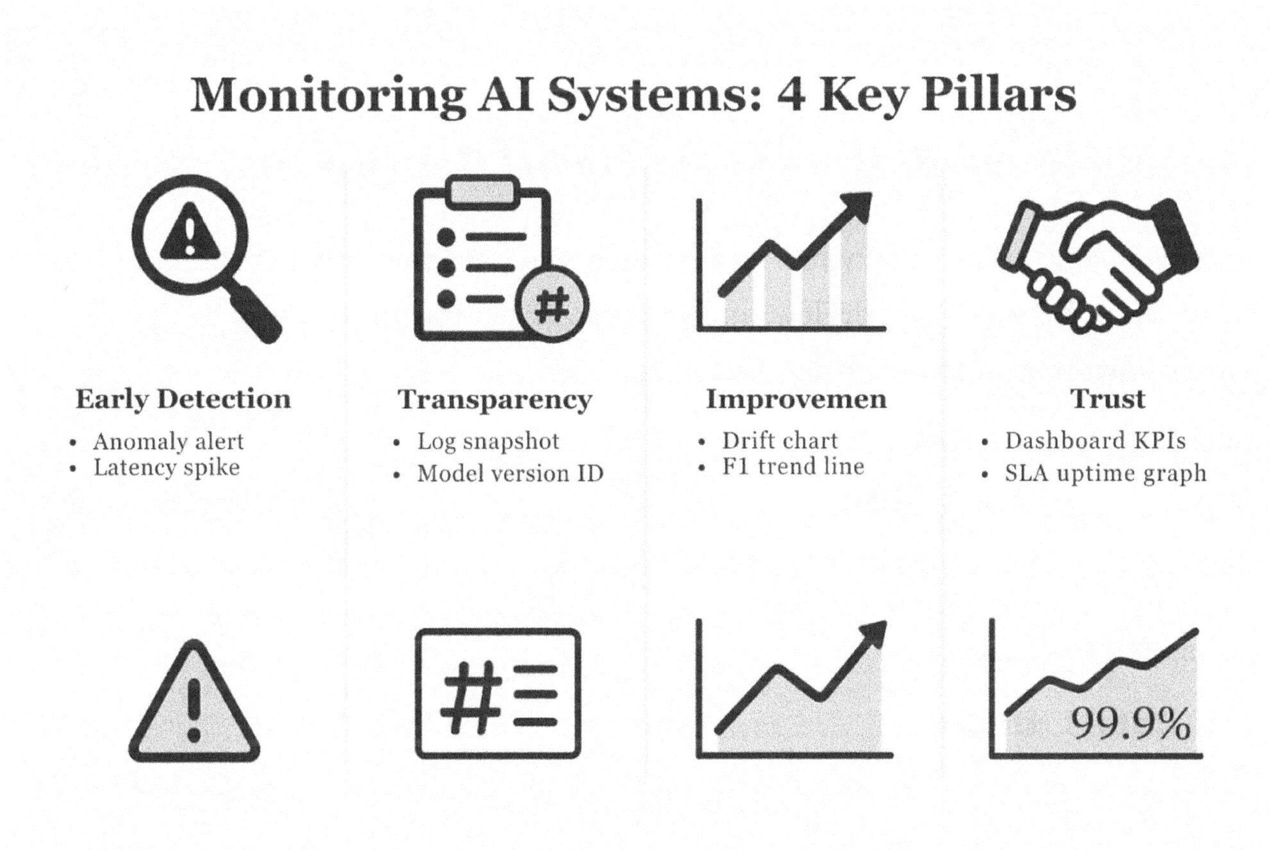

Robust monitoring infrastructure marks the difference between experimental AI and production-grade systems. It enables:

- Early detection of failure
- Complete system auditability

- Continuous, measurable improvement
- Trust from every stakeholder

In the next section, we'll dive into **MLflow's** tracking capabilities and show how to scale this monitoring strategy across your workflows—turning observability into a strategic advantage.

Getting Started: How to Set Up MLflow for Your Project

MLflow is compatible with Python 3.7 and later, and integrates well with libraries like scikit-learn, XGBoost, TensorFlow, and PyTorch. To get started, create and activate a virtual environment to isolate dependencies:

```
python -m venv .venv
source .venv/bin/activate  # On Windows use .venv\Scripts\activate
```

Install MLflow using pip:

```
pip install mlflow
```

If you're using scikit-learn, add:

```
pip install scikit-learn
```

If installation fails due to wheel build issues, upgrade pip or install build tools (e.g., gcc on Linux or Visual Studio Build Tools on Windows).

Next, organize your project by adding a directory to store MLflow run metadata and artifacts:

```
mkdir mlflow_runs
```

Use the following project structure to keep everything organized:

```
project_root/
├── src/
│   └── <your_code>.py
├── mlflow_runs/
└── requirements.txt
```

To launch MLflow's UI:

```
mlflow ui --backend-store-uri ./mlflow_runs
```

Visit `http://localhost:5000` in your browser to explore experiment runs and artifacts. If the default port is busy, specify another with `--port 5001`.

Understanding Core Concepts

- **Experiments**: Group related runs.
- **Runs**: Store metadata for individual training/evaluation sessions.
- **Parameters**: Logged input values.
- **Metrics**: Validation results.
- **Artifacts**: Files such as models and plots.

Each run allows logging of parameters, metrics, and artifacts, enabling easy comparison between iterations.

Example: Iris Classifier with scikit-learn

```
import mlflow
import mlflow.sklearn
from sklearn.datasets import load_iris
from sklearn.model_selection import train_test_split
from sklearn.linear_model import LogisticRegression
from sklearn.metrics import accuracy_score

mlflow.set_experiment("Iris_Classifier")

data = load_iris()
X_train, X_test, y_train, y_test = train_test_split(data.data,
data.target, test_size=0.2)

with mlflow.start_run():
    learning_rate = 0.01
    mlflow.log_param("learning_rate", learning_rate)
    clf = LogisticRegression(C=1/learning_rate, max_iter=200)
    clf.fit(X_train, y_train)
    predictions = clf.predict(X_test)
    acc = accuracy_score(y_test, predictions)
    mlflow.log_metric("accuracy", acc)
    mlflow.sklearn.log_model(clf, "model")
    print(f"Logged run with accuracy: {acc:.3f}")
```

After running the script, reload the MLflow UI to view your "Iris_Classifier" experiment. You'll see run details including timestamp, parameters, metrics, and model artifacts ready for download.

Troubleshooting Installation

If you encounter errors:

```
pip install --upgrade pip setuptools wheel
```

- On Linux: `sudo apt install build-essential`
- On Windows: Install Visual Studio Build Tools

Final Thoughts

This setup ensures reproducibility and clean experiment tracking, supporting future migration to remote MLflow servers. It also lays the groundwork for advanced logging: per-epoch metrics, nested runs, and custom artifact logging—crucial for long-term AI system reliability.

Logging What Counts: Capturing Model Metrics in MLflow

Tracking model performance over time is critical for real-world AI workflows. MLflow's tracking API enables structured, repeatable logging of key metrics such as accuracy, loss, and custom evaluation logic.

Start by wrapping your training logic inside an MLflow run to ensure metrics, parameters, and artifacts are recorded under a unified execution context. Here's an example for classification:

```
import mlflow
from sklearn.ensemble import RandomForestClassifier
from sklearn.metrics import accuracy_score, log_loss
from sklearn.model_selection import train_test_split
import pandas as pd

# Load and split dataset
data = pd.read_csv("classification_data.csv")
X = data.drop(columns=["target"])
y = data["target"]
X_train, X_test, y_train, y_test = train_test_split(X, y,
test_size=0.2, random_state=42)

try:
    with mlflow.start_run():
        model = RandomForestClassifier(n_estimators=100,
random_state=42)
```

```
        model.fit(X_train, y_train)
        y_pred = model.predict(X_test)
        y_pred_proba = model.predict_proba(X_test)

        acc = accuracy_score(y_test, y_pred)
        loss = log_loss(y_test, y_pred_proba)

        mlflow.log_metric("accuracy", acc)
        mlflow.log_metric("log_loss", loss)
        mlflow.set_tag("model_type", "RandomForestClassifier")
except Exception as e:
    print(f"MLflow Logging Error: {e}")
```

In the MLflow UI, each run logs accuracy, log loss, timestamps, and model tags—making it easy to compare and track improvements.

Logging for Regression

Regression tasks use similar patterns, logging different metrics:

```
from sklearn.linear_model import LinearRegression
from sklearn.metrics import mean_squared_error, mean_absolute_error

try:
  with mlflow.start_run():
    reg = LinearRegression()
    reg.fit(X_train, y_train)
    preds = reg.predict(X_test)
```

```
        mse = mean_squared_error(y_test, preds)
        mae = mean_absolute_error(y_test, preds)

        mlflow.log_metric("mean_squared_error", mse)
        mlflow.log_metric("mean_absolute_error", mae)
        mlflow.set_tag("problem_type", "regression")
except Exception as err:
    print(f"Regression Logging Failed: {err}")
```

MLflow immediately displays these metrics, making it simple to filter and compare runs.

Logging Custom Metrics

You can log any custom metric, like Matthews Correlation Coefficient (MCC):

```
from sklearn.metrics import matthews_corrcoef

try:
    with mlflow.start_run():
        mcc = matthews_corrcoef(y_test, y_pred)
        mlflow.log_metric("matthews_corrcoef", mcc)
except Exception as e:
    print(f"Custom Metric Logging Error: {e}")
```

Dataset Versioning

For better reproducibility, MLflow also supports dataset version tracking:

```
import mlflow.data
```

```
try:
    dataset_src = mlflow.data.from_pandas(
        df=X_train,
        source="s3://your-bucket/dataset.csv",
        name="training-data-v1"
    )
    mlflow.log_input(dataset_src, context="training")
    mlflow.log_param("dataset_version", "v1.2")
except Exception as e:
    print(f"Dataset Logging Error: {e}")
```

These practices align data, code, and results for seamless development-to-production transitions.

Once metrics and inputs are logged, MLflow's UI groups and visualizes them automatically. These artifacts form the basis for dashboards and comparative analytics—enabling informed decisions and continuous optimization.

Visualizing Success: Analyzing Results with MLflow Tools

MLflow's dashboard tools let teams monitor key metrics and identify trends quickly. In the Tracking UI, navigate to your experiment, open the "Charts" or "Visualize" tab, and select metrics like accuracy, loss, or F1 score. Use the filter bar to isolate runs by tag, parameter, or user. Saved searches allow customized views—helpful for role-based dashboards such as "Model Metrics" for data scientists or "KPI Summary" for executives.

Customizing Dashboards for Team Role

Click "Configure Columns" to personalize tables, highlight important columns, and use "Group by" to organize runs by model type or dataset version. Add "Comparison" views to inspect runs side by side. Data scientists might focus on hyperparameters and validation loss; managers might prioritize deployment readiness and business impact. Save each view with clear labels for quick access.

Filtering, Grouping, and Navigating Data

Use advanced filters in the search bar, such as `params.optimizer = 'adam'`, to target specific configurations. Combine filters with logical operators (e.g., `params.batch_size = 32 AND tags.build = 'production'`). Group runs by any parameter or tag to surface trends within similar experiment families. Switch between grouped and ungrouped views to toggle between summary and detailed data.

Building Comparative Plots and Multi-Model Analyses

Use the "Compare" feature to visualize metrics across multiple runs. Create line or bar plots comparing accuracy, loss, or custom KPIs. For example, visualize how batch size or learning rate impacts model performance. Compare architectures—e.g., CNN vs. ResNet—on metrics like validation loss or inference time. Add notes for context and collaborative decision-making.

Longitudinal Trend Analysis with Plotting

Track progress by plotting metrics over time. Select a metric (e.g., accuracy), set the X-axis to time or epoch, and enable smoothing to clarify trends. Use this to identify regressions (spikes), improvements (upward curves), or stagnation (plateaus). These insights guide tuning and help prioritize experiments.

Generating and Customizing Shareable Reports

Export dashboards via the “Export” button—choose HTML or PDF. Include visuals, filtered tables, and metric comparisons. For technical reports, embed raw data, hyperparameter grids, and annotations. For executives, highlight business outcomes and next steps. Share reports via email or internal platforms to keep all stakeholders informed.

By mastering these visualization tools, teams accelerate iteration, enhance transparency, and connect experimentation to strategic goals.

Closing the Loop: Iteration Strategies for Smarter AI Monitoring

Monitoring insights provide the foundation for continuous improvement in AI projects. By collecting targeted data throughout the model lifecycle, teams can react quickly to performance issues, optimize features, and drive progress with structured feedback loops.

Feedback-Driven Model Tuning

When a classification model underperforms due to data drift, MLflow dashboards can highlight drops in precision or recall. Feature importance logs help pinpoint failing segments. Teams then use historic runs to tune hyperparameters and validate improvements.

```
import mlflow
from mlflow.tracking import MlflowClient

client = MlflowClient()
runs = client.search_runs(experiment_ids=["0"], filter_string="metrics.auc < 0.8")
for run in runs:
    print(f"Run {run.info.run_id} - Learning Rate: {run.data.params['lr']}, AUC: {run.data.metrics['auc']}")
```

Using this information, teams can adjust regularization or learning rate, then monitor improvements in future runs. This iterative process—identify, adjust, validate—drives consistent accuracy gains and process maturity.

Anomaly Detection Systems

To prevent failures, MLflow tracks custom metrics like latency spikes or feature drift. Thresholds are defined using historic averages. Breaches can trigger alerts via tools like Slack or PagerDuty:

```
alerts:
  - metric: latency
    threshold: 500
    action: notify_slack
```

Integrating observability tools (e.g., Datadog) with MLflow boosts detection accuracy. Teams review false positives monthly to recalibrate thresholds and reduce alert fatigue.

Documentation Best Practices

Document each tuning cycle with standardized templates:

```
#### Experiment: Increased L2 Regularization
- Date: 2024-04-15
- Hypothesis: Reducing overfitting by increasing regularization
- Baseline AUC: 0.772
- New AUC: 0.804
- Data Version: v1.13
- Notes: Improvement in segment X, minor drop in recall for segment Y
```

Store logs in a centralized location linked to MLflow run IDs. This improves transparency, onboarding, and institutional knowledge.

Review Process Implementation

Teams hold regular review sessions to assess MLflow dashboards. Outliers trigger root-cause analysis and task creation. For example, a precision drop in a customer segment might lead to a backlog item for retraining. Impact assessments guide prioritization: high-risk issues take precedence, while lower risks enter future sprints.

Structured reviews and cross-team training lead to better code quality and more reliable models—transforming monitoring insights into continuous value.

Bringing It All Together

By now, it's clear how monitoring underpins robust AI development—and how MLflow empowers that process through tracking, visualization, and continuous feedback. Armed with these tools and techniques, teams can proactively detect issues, maintain full auditability, and iterate with confidence.

These practices not only boost performance and reliability but also build trust among stakeholders. Whether scaling to production or experimenting with new models, MLflow becomes the backbone of a sustainable AI workflow.

Going forward, applying these strategies will be essential for teams building real-world AI systems ready for deployment and scale.

Chapter 8

From Projects to Paychecks: Using Your Work to Land AI Jobs

How do you turn AI projects into real job opportunities? What makes a portfolio stand out in a crowded market? How do you clearly explain your work in interviews to demonstrate not just technical skill but tangible impact?

This chapter walks you through transforming AI projects into compelling tools for career advancement. You'll learn how to build an attention-grabbing GitHub portfolio, communicate project value during interviews, and optimize profiles like LinkedIn and your CV. We also cover managing applications, preparing for technical and behavioral interviews, and staying competitive after landing your first role.

Building a Standout GitHub Portfolio

Presenting your AI work effectively on GitHub can open doors to interviews and job offers. Recruiters often judge a project at a glance, so clear structure, strong documentation, and evidence of success are crucial. Discoverability is just as important as presentation—especially for technical hiring managers.

Repository Naming

A repository's name is your first chance to communicate purpose. Favor descriptive, keyword-rich titles over cryptic or playful ones. For example:

- ✓ `object-detection-yolov8-pytorch`

- ✓ `sentiment-analysis-bert-finetuning`
- ✓ `fraud-detection-xgboost-credit-card-transactions`
- ✗ `SuperNetV2`
- ✗ `ProjectX_2024`
- ✗ `MLFinal`

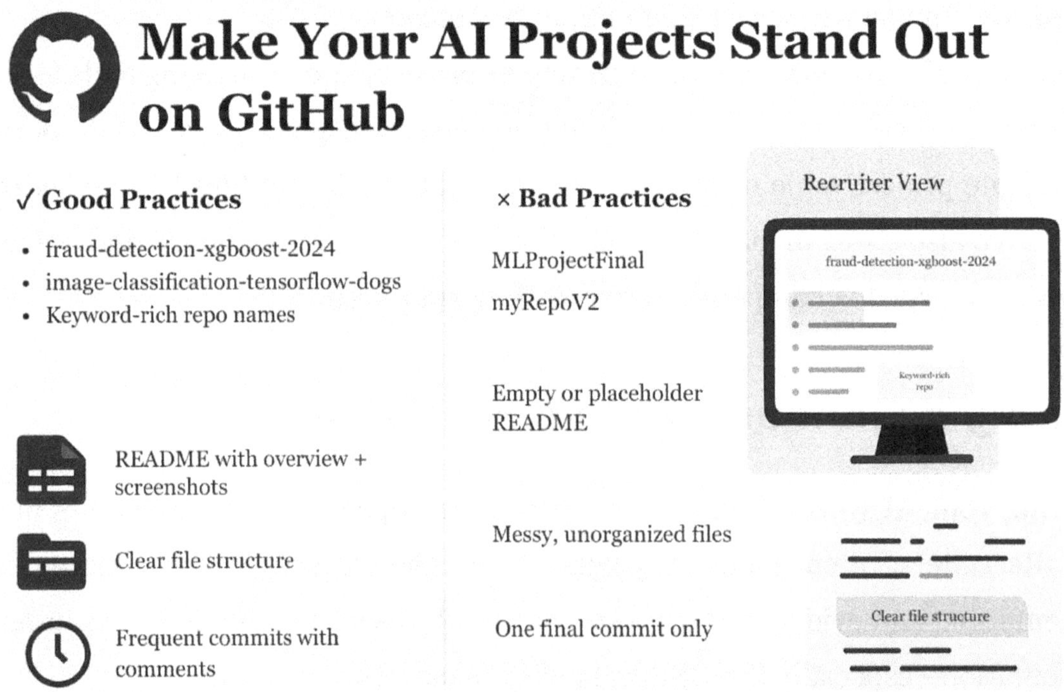

The goal is to make it obvious what the project does, what tools it uses, and what domain it targets. If you're working with classification and TensorFlow, a name like `image-classification-tensorflow-cats-vs-dogs` makes this immediately clear.

This approach improves visibility in search results and ensures technical stakeholders understand your skills at a glance.

README Documentation

The README is your elevator pitch. It should clearly express the project's intent, highlight its impact, and guide users through usage—all in a professional, approachable tone.

Here's an effective opening:

This repository contains a BERT-based model for identifying user intent in customer support tickets. The model achieved 92% intent classification accuracy on a public e-commerce dataset.

Key Components:

- **Project Overview**: Summarize the AI task, approach, and results.
- **Technologies Used**: Include clear tech tags (e.g., TensorFlow, HuggingFace, Docker).
- **Installation**:

  ```
  pip install -r requirements.txt
  python app.py
  ```

- **Usage**:

  ```
  python predict.py --input sample.txt
  ```

- **Unique Features**: Briefly mention enhancements like "Implements Mixup augmentation" or "Includes TensorBoard logging."

- **Troubleshooting & Feedback**: Common issues and contact info show professionalism.

Use markdown for clarity without clutter. Supplement with lightweight visuals (charts, screenshots, or small GIFs).

Demo Materials

Demo assets provide instant clarity. A short (<1 min) GIF or video showing "input → model → output" is often enough.

For technical demos, use cleanly organized Jupyter notebooks. Include:

- Markdown headers (Intro, Training, Inference)
- Code/output cells together (charts, confusion matrices)
- Top-of-notebook setup: dependencies, Python version, resource needs

Link to Colab or Hugging Face Spaces where applicable.

Commit History Management

Your Git history reveals how you think. Keep commits focused, atomic, and descriptive:

- ✓ `added data preprocessing pipeline`
- ✓ `implemented GRU model for forecasting`
- ✓ `refactored training loop, improved validation accuracy`

Avoid vague or batch commits like:

- ✗ `stuff`
- ✗ `final update`

- ✗ `misc fixes`

A healthy commit flow might look like:

```
[Init] add base directory & requirements.txt
Add exploratory data analysis notebook
Implement GRU-based model for time series
Refactor training loop for efficiency
Add evaluation script, update README with metrics
```

Use branches for experiments and merge cleanly to reflect real-world collaboration practices.

Projects that are well-named, well-documented, and versioned professionally not only attract recruiter interest—they set you up for confident interviews and long-term credibility.

Showcasing Projects in Interviews

Communicating Impact

Effectively presenting AI projects in job interviews begins with clearly establishing their real-world value. Framing projects by the business problem they address helps interviewers connect your work to outcomes that matter. For example:
"By implementing an automated document review system, I reduced contract analysis time by 75% compared to manual processing."

For industry-specific relevance:

"Developed a fraud-detection model that cut false positives by 30%, supporting safer customer transactions."

Research the employer and connect your achievements to their domain. Example:

"Optimized route prediction increased fleet efficiency by 18%, relevant to your logistics AI platform."

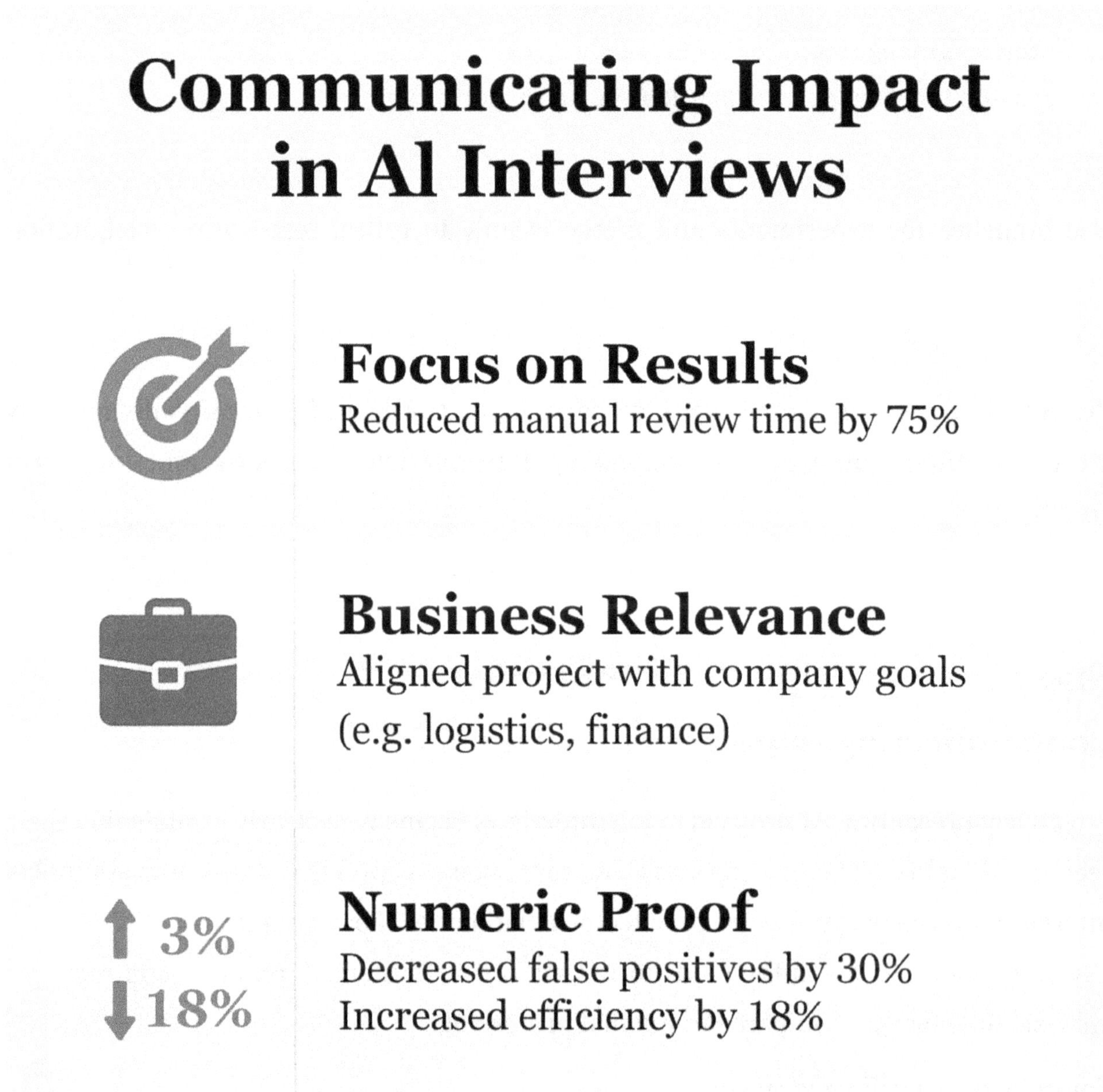

Quantifying Results

Use specific metrics:

- "Lowered defect rates by 15% using computer vision."
- "Reduced moderation cycles by 50% via a robust text classifier."

These figures provide clear proof of value.

Technical Discussion

Avoid jargon. Structure explanations by high-level decisions, then add detail:
"We chose Random Forests over Logistic Regression for nonlinear pattern detection, reducing false negatives by 10%."
Sample statements:

- "Grid search tuning raised our F1 score from 0.72 to 0.81."
- "We prioritized inference speed, selecting MobileNet over ResNet."

Break down concepts clearly:

"We cleaned the data, trained models, used cross-validation, then selected the most efficient pipeline."

Crafting Project Narratives

Structure answers as:

- **Situation**: "Onboarding delays were hurting conversion."
- **Task**: "Build a document parser."
- **Action**: "Implemented OCR + rules-based NLP."
- **Result**: "Reduced onboarding time by 60%."

Highlight turning points:
"When false positives spiked, I re-labeled data, improving precision by 20%."

Preparing for Demos

Identify project highlights (dashboards, scripts, notebooks). Rehearse walkthroughs. Prepare slides with:

- Project goal
- Visual summary of results
- Backup screenshots in case of tech issues

Have contingency plans:

"If the model fails to load, I'll walk through key steps manually and explain debugging."

Outline clearly:

- The original problem
- Your solution steps
- Measurable outcomes

This builds credibility and shows composure under pressure—crucial in fast-paced, AI-driven workplaces.

Optimizing Your LinkedIn and CV for AI Roles

Start by reviewing multiple AI job postings and listing recurring keywords such as "`machine learning pipeline`," "model interpretability," "cloud deployment," or "PyTorch." Then naturally integrate these terms into your LinkedIn summary, skills, and experience sections.

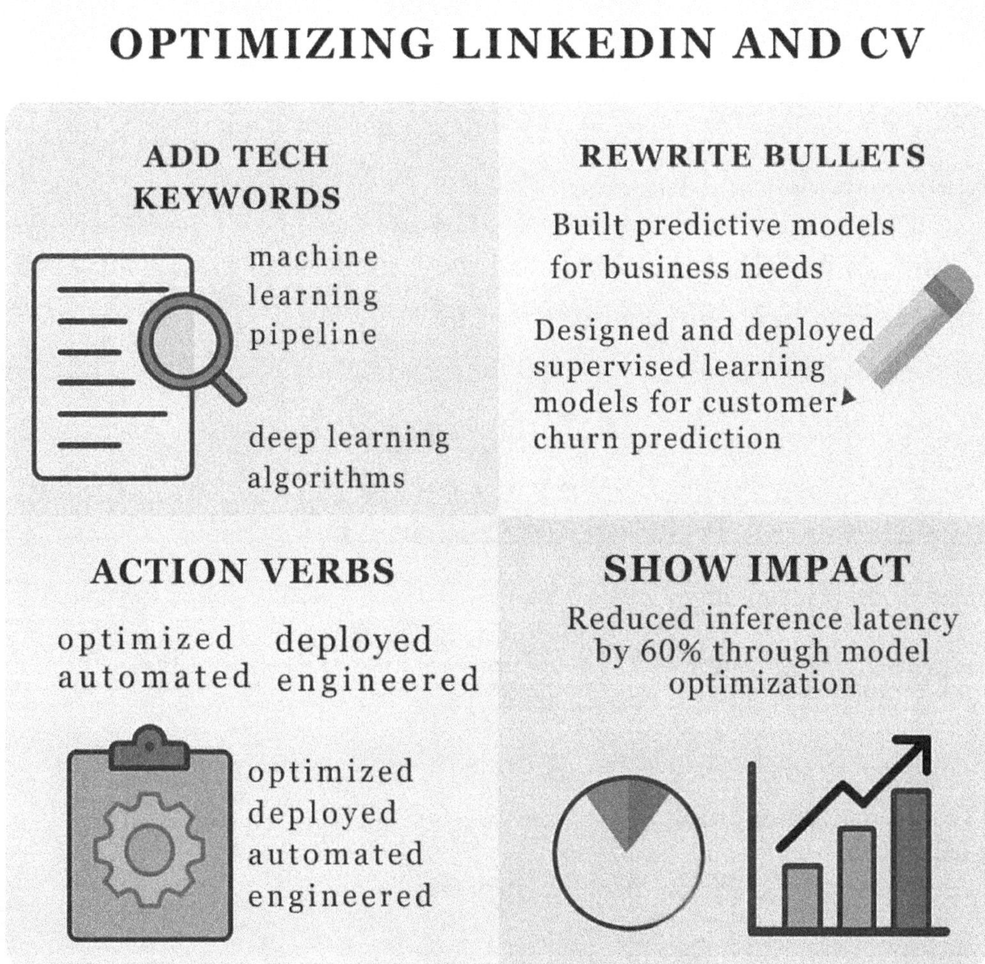

Integrating AI Keywords into Your Profile

Instead of vague phrases like:

- "Built predictive models for business needs"

Refine with specificity:

- "Designed and deployed supervised learning models for churn prediction using Python and Scikit-learn"

Add context through tools and outcomes:

- "Developed scalable ETL pipelines and preprocessing routines in Python/SQL for high-volume datasets"

Project Features and Action Verbs for AI

Use impact-oriented language:

- "Optimized," "Automated," "Engineered," "Integrated"

Combine results with outcomes:

- "Reduced latency by 60% via model compression"
- "Automated retraining pipeline, cutting deployment time by 30%"
- "Increased fraud detection accuracy from 82% to 91% using PyTorch ensemble models"

- "Built TensorBoard and Grafana dashboards for proactive monitoring, reducing downtime 45%"

Format each role or project with 2–4 bullet points, clearly linking work to user or business impact.

Showcasing Projects on LinkedIn

Use the Featured section to add:

1. PDFs summarizing your AI projects with visuals
2. GitHub links to code and notebooks
3. Blog posts explaining problem-solving steps
4. Demo videos or walkthroughs

Describe each item concisely:

```
"Built Transformer-based summarizer; raised F1 from 0.63 to 0.74. Full
writeup and source code below."
```

Update regularly with awards, new projects, and presentations.

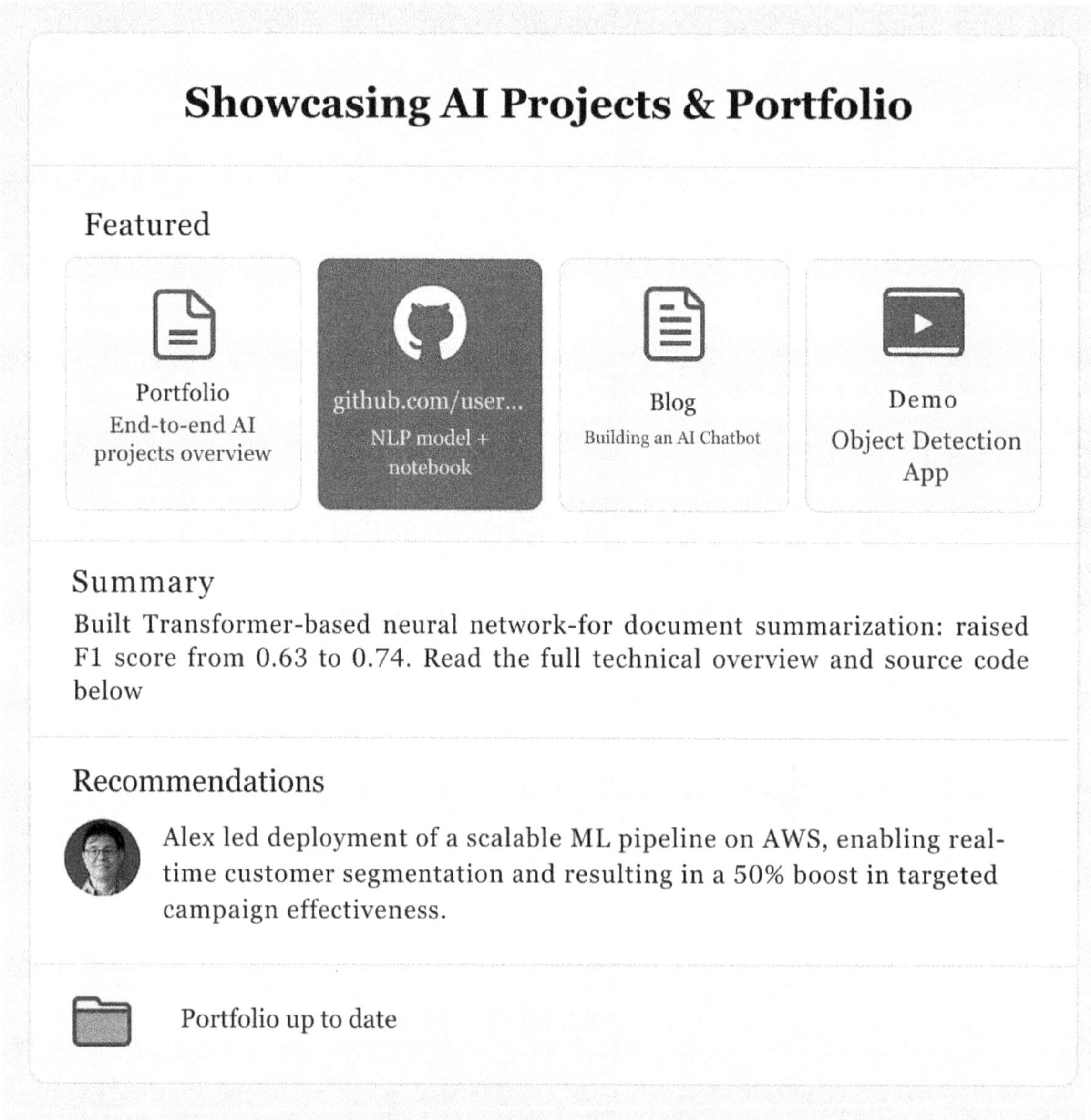

Gaining Strong Endorsements and Recommendations

Place top AI skills like "`Machine Learning,`" "`TensorFlow`," or "`Model Deployment`" in your Skills section. Limit to 10 targeted competencies.

Ask mentors or collaborators to endorse and recommend with focus:

```
"Can you mention my work on the fraud pipeline and monthly data audits?"
```

Strong examples:

```
"Alex deployed a scalable ML pipeline on AWS, improving campaign ROI by 50%."
```

Regularly refresh your profile to reflect new certifications, tools, and measurable results.

The AI Career Kit: Turbocharged Applications

Getting noticed by employers in AI starts with targeted outreach using the right tools. Recruiter emails should be direct and tailored, connecting your key projects with the employer's needs. For maximum impact, include a focused subject line, a brief introduction explaining your interest and connection to the company, two lines highlighting a project or accomplishment relevant to the job posting, and a sentence explaining why you're pursuing them in particular. End with a prompt for next steps. For example:

```
Subject: AI Engineer Application – [Your Name]
Hi [Recruiter Name],
I'm an AI developer passionate about deploying machine learning in healthcare. My recent project, [Project Title], improved diagnostic accuracy at [Company/University Lab]. I was excited to see your opening for an AI Engineer at [Company], as my experience closely matches your requirements, especially in deploying models at scale. I'd love to discuss how I can contribute to your team's goals. When would be a good time to connect?
```

```
Best regards,
[Your Name]
[LinkedIn/GitHub link]
```

To ensure you don't lose track of opportunities, an application tracking checklist is crucial. This checklist should include fields such as Company Name, Position, Date

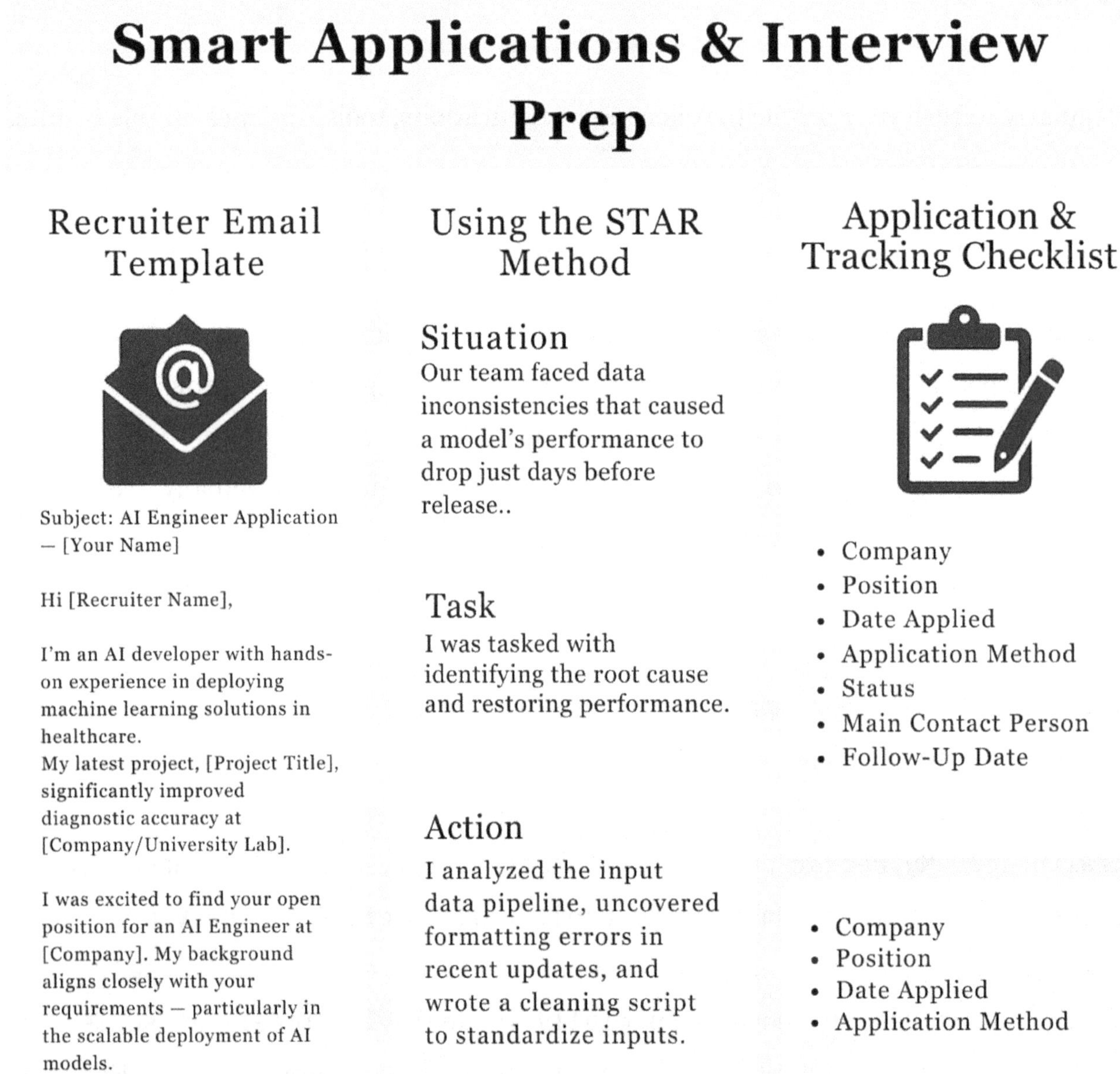

Applied, Application Method, Status (Applied/Interview/Offer/Rejected), Key Contact, and Follow-up Dates. A mock entry looks like this:

- `Company: HealthAI Solutions`
- `Role: Data Scientist`
- `Date Applied: 2025-04-15`
- `Application Method: Company Portal`
- `Status: Interview`
- `Key Contact: Jamie Lee (jamie.lee@healthai.com)`
- `Follow-up Date: 2025-04-22`

Application tracking systems like Teamtailor and Teal's Job Application Tracker help to automate reminders, track status changes, and synthesize insights about where your applications have the greatest traction.

During interviews, behavioral questions evaluate how you solve problems and collaborate. Prepare STAR (Situation, Task, Action, Result) responses for these essential questions:

1. Tell me about a time you solved a difficult technical problem.
2. Describe a project where you worked under tight deadlines.
3. Give an example of how you handled team conflict.
4. Share a situation where you took initiative in an AI project.

A complete STAR response for the first question:

- **Situation**: Our team faced data inconsistencies that caused a model's performance to drop just days before release.
- **Task**: I was tasked with identifying the root cause and restoring performance.
- **Action**: I analyzed the input data pipeline, uncovered formatting errors in recent updates, and wrote a cleaning script to standardize inputs.
- **Result**: The model's accuracy improved by 15%, and we launched on schedule, earning team recognition.

Having versions of your STAR stories allows you to adapt them during interviews, whether the question focuses on technical skills, teamwork, or leadership. Review your responses regularly using platforms like Pramp and Interviewing.io for mock interviews.

Salary negotiation often feels daunting, but using clear scripts improves your confidence. When you receive an offer, politely ask for time to review, research average salaries for the role using Glassdoor, Levels.fyi, or Payscale, then initiate negotiation with this approach:

You: Thank you for the offer. Based on my research and the responsibilities of the AI Engineer position, I was expecting a salary in the $110k-$125k range. Is there flexibility to align the offer more closely with current market rates?

Recruiter: We appreciate your feedback. We might be able to adjust slightly.

You: I appreciate that. In addition to salary, could we also discuss a signing bonus or additional PTO?

Handling objections involves restating your value and willingness to be flexible:

Recruiter: Our budget is limited.

You: I understand and am excited about your team. Is there room for growth in compensation after six months based on performance?

Making templates and checklists personal but efficient means adjusting details—such as referencing company values, using keywords from job postings, and customizing STAR examples for specific company projects. Application pattern analysis reveals which types of applications receive the most callbacks, enabling smarter strategy tweaks. Use visually consistent documents and adapt STAR stories to keep your narrative clear yet pliable. Avoid the temptation to over-customize and risk losing authenticity.

Set daily targets—apply to three jobs per day or 10–15 per week. Track an outreach response rate of at least 20%, and dedicate 3–5 days to preparing for each round of interviews. Salary ranges for entry-level AI roles typically span $90k–$120k, while senior engineers command $130k–$170k, depending on region and company.

By methodically applying these tools—efficient outreach, consistent tracking, strong behavioral prep, and assertive negotiation—you set yourself on a trajectory for ongoing growth and opportunity discovery in the AI field.

Staying Relevant: Learning and Growing Past

Staying Informed and Engaged with the Industry

The rapid evolution of AI makes awareness of current trends, tools, and breakthroughs essential for career growth. Rather than just browsing headlines, professionals can build a habit of following established sources and engaging with their communities. Subscribing to newsletters like *The Batch* (from deeplearning.ai), *Import AI*, or *O'Reilly's AI newsletter* provides a curated flow of research highlights and product announcements. Set aside thirty minutes each week to read the latest issues, then reflect on new ideas or technologies that could enhance your work. Extend learning by commenting on articles or joining newsletter-associated community forums such as Reddit's r/MachineLearning or LinkedIn discussion threads. Ask questions or share a brief takeaway from your experience applying a technique mentioned in a recent article. These actions encourage deeper understanding and visibility among peers, reinforcing a cycle of growth and network-building (Fauvel, 2025).

Curating and Evolving Your Portfolio

An up-to-date portfolio signals relevance and commitment to growth. Create a quarterly review schedule—mark the start of each new quarter to review and update your GitHub repositories or personal website. Add new projects that demonstrate skills in trending areas such as generative AI or responsible AI, reflecting current industry priorities (Loh et al., 2024). Before adding a project, ask if it aligns with your evolving interests or fills a skills gap. For each project, write a brief summary highlighting the problem, your solution, and the impact achieved.

Evaluate existing projects using criteria like code quality, up-to-dateness with recent frameworks, relevance to current roles, and feedback received from colleagues or online reviewers. Remove projects that use outdated libraries, lack clear documentation, or do not demonstrate skills relevant to your targeted roles. Instead of keeping every side project, showcase two to four that represent your best and most recent work. For instance, when moving into responsible AI, replace old classification demo scripts with explainability dashboards or bias analysis case studies (Loh et al., 2024).

Integrate learnings from industry newsletters—such as a new optimization method featured in a blog—into a real portfolio project. Document what inspired your refinement, and include links or short commentary in your project README to show active engagement with industry trends (Fauvel, 2025).

Networking and Building Community Relationships

Strategic networking extends beyond collecting contacts on LinkedIn. Identify target professionals and organizations using tools like Meetup, Eventbrite, or major Slack/Discord channels focused on AI (such as DataTalks.Club or the MLOps Community). Select one to three relevant communities and participate in discussions twice a month, sharing resources, asking for advice, and volunteering to help with group projects.

Seek out mentors using platforms like ADPList or the mentorship sections on Women in AI or Black in AI. Draft a concise, personalized message outlining what drew you to their profile, your professional goals, and one specific skill you hope to develop. A direct ask like, "Would you be willing to chat about scalable model deployment strategies for 20 minutes?" is more effective than a generic request for mentorship.

Contributing to open-source projects, even with modest pull requests or by writing documentation, creates meaningful interactions. Such contributions foster reciprocity and let you learn collaboratively, building connections with experienced practitioners who can later provide job referrals or feedback on your work.

Measure network engagement by tracking the number of meaningful conversations each month, the quality of responses received to your questions or advice, and the frequency with which new contacts invite you to collaborate or share resources.

Structuring and Tracking Learning Goals

Professional growth flourishes with clearly defined, measurable learning targets. At the start of each quarter, select two technical topics that advance your core skill set—such as prompt engineering for generative AI or implementing AI fairness checks—and set deadlines. For example, "Deploy a multi-model inference API using FastAPI and Docker by the end of this quarter."

Break larger topics into weekly learning sprints. If you plan to master AI interpretability tools, outline a four-week roadmap: week 1—read the SHAP and LIME documentation and tutorials; week 2—build a toy project on a public dataset; week 3—implement advanced features or combine methods; week 4—write a blog post or update your portfolio to showcase the output.

Track progress with tools like Notion, Trello, or a bullet journal. Co-ordinate milestone reviews with trusted peers or mentors for regular feedback. Celebrate completions—such as earning a micro-credential from Coursera or publishing a new portfolio piece—by sharing reflections with your network or writing a LinkedIn post.

Establish recurring check-ins to adjust your learning plan based on project demands or industry shifts highlighted in newsletters. The ability to adapt, document mastery, and share what you learn closes the loop between learning and professional advancement. These habits help ensure that AI professionals remain agile, in-demand, and fulfilled in an ever-changing workplace (Fauvel, 2025; Loh et al., 2024).

Continuous Learning & Networking

AI Learning Sources
newsletters, forums

Quarterly Goals
tracking tools

Mentorship
industry mentors

Open-Source Contributions:
code, docs

Bringing It All Together

Now that you have a clear roadmap for building standout portfolios, presenting your projects effectively in interviews, optimizing your professional profiles, and navigating job applications with practical tools, you are well-equipped to transform your AI work into compelling career opportunities. By applying these strategies, you can confidently demonstrate your skills, communicate the impact of your projects, and engage with employers in a way that highlights your readiness for AI roles. Moving forward, continue refining your portfolio, honing your interview narratives, and maintaining an active learning mindset to stay relevant and grow steadily in the fast-evolving AI landscape. This proactive approach will help you not only secure your first AI job but also build a sustainable, rewarding career.

Conclusion

As you reach the end of this book, pause to reflect on how far you've come since that first page. This journey was never simply about learning a technology or memorizing a set of tools—it was a guided transformation designed to empower you as a confident, job-ready AI engineer. Every chapter, exercise, and project was crafted to move you from curiosity to capability, equipping you not just to understand artificial intelligence, but to apply it, deploy it, and ultimately shape the future with it.

From the outset, you embarked on a hands-on learning path built for real-world results. The practical, project-first approach has done more than fill your toolkit; it has enabled you to think like a builder, solve problems like an engineer, and adapt like a professional in a rapidly evolving field. By following these steps and engaging deeply with each project, you have learned how to transform theoretical knowledge into tangible, marketable skills—skills that stand out in today's competitive AI landscape.

Throughout this book, we demystified the discipline of AI engineering. You learned that mastering AI extends beyond algorithms and models—it's about nurturing a mindset oriented toward building, experimenting, and continuously improving. Rather than focusing solely on abstract concepts, you tackled meaningful projects that addressed authentic challenges. Each milestone contributed to a cohesive narrative: gaining proficiency with foundational modern tools like OpenAI API, HuggingFace, FastAPI, Docker, and MLflow; understanding how these technologies interconnect; and leveraging them to power real, deployable AI systems.

Understanding toolchains wasn't presented as an isolated task. Instead, you saw how each element forms part of the comprehensive framework required for long-term career growth. Building a sentiment analysis pipeline, deploying models using containers, architecting scalable, production-ready APIs—each step layered new knowledge upon the last, connecting theory to action and reinforcing your ability to create value in any AI environment.

By emphasizing breakthrough insights, this book aimed to set you apart. One of the most crucial lessons is that project-based learning consistently outpaces theory-driven study when it comes to readiness for real jobs. Books and lectures provide foundations, but it is hands-on work that cements expertise and generates proof of skill. In completing end-to-end projects—and not shying away from deployment, monitoring, and iteration—you've learned how to deliver AI solutions that work not just in notebooks, but in the real world where users depend on reliability and scalability.

You now appreciate the impact of model fine-tuning, especially in niche domains where general solutions often fall short. The experience of selecting data, customizing models, and evaluating performance has given you practical insight into one of the most valuable areas of modern AI. And by assembling a well-crafted portfolio—a record not only of what you have built, but also of how you solved problems, learned from failures, and iterated toward excellence—you hold a career asset that can open doors and accelerate your transition from learner to practitioner.

The path you've walked has not been easy. Progressing through this material has demanded attention, persistence, and adaptability. Many of you balanced learning with demanding schedules, overcame technical hurdles, and pushed through moments of frustration. It is important to recognize the commitment these efforts represent.

Completing these projects and chapters is an achievement worth celebrating. Take pride in how much ground you have covered and know that every challenge met along the way has prepared you for the demands of professional AI engineering.

But the journey does not end here. Sustained momentum is key in a fast-moving world. As you move forward, make a habit of updating your portfolio regularly with new projects and novel ideas. Engage actively with vibrant AI communities—whether online, at conferences, or within local meetups. Stay attuned to emerging trends, upcoming tools, and best practices. Set clear personal goals to ensure continuous learning, and, wherever possible, align your self-directed projects with the tasks and needs you encounter in professional settings. Integrating ongoing experimentation with real work will deepen your mastery and keep your expertise current as the field evolves.

Importantly, do not pursue this path in isolation. One of the most effective ways to reinforce your own knowledge, gain feedback, and cultivate new opportunities is to share your progress and insights openly. Contribute to open-source projects, write blog posts or tutorials, participate in study groups, or showcase your work on professional networks. These acts of sharing are not mere extracurriculars—they are central to building a supportive network and advancing both personal and community-driven progress in AI engineering. By helping others learn, you strengthen your own understanding and contribute to a culture of accessible, practical AI education.

Thank you sincerely for choosing this book as your guide and for investing your time and energy in building your skills. Your willingness to engage with complex ideas, confront difficult challenges, and persist where others might stop places you among a new generation of AI engineers. Your journey represents not just personal advancement, but participation in a broader movement to make powerful, responsible AI accessible and usable across industries, applications, and communities.

Now, as you look ahead, I encourage you to take full ownership of your career trajectory. The roadmap outlined here—from foundational principles to deployment, from tool mastery to impactful portfolios—is proven and reliable, yet the driving force behind ongoing success is your initiative and adaptability. Approach each new project with confidence, knowing that you possess both the technical foundation and the practical experience to navigate uncertainty and overcome obstacles. Adopt the mindset of a lifelong explorer: experiment boldly, learn relentlessly, and embrace challenges as gateways to deeper understanding and greater impact.

Remember, the AI field is dynamic, shaped daily by innovation and discovery. Curiosity and continuous learning are your greatest assets. See this book not as an endpoint, but as a launch pad—a solid foundation on which to build, refine, and extend your expertise indefinitely. With the skills, mindset, and sense of community you have developed, you are ready not just to keep pace with AI's evolution, but to help lead it, inspire others, and contribute meaningfully to the future.

Your journey as an AI engineer is truly just beginning. Carry forward the perseverance, resourcefulness, and collaborative spirit fostered here. Own your path, support others, and keep building. The next breakthrough—even the next great leap in AI—might start with your very next project.

Your Next Step to Real-World AI

You've just gained the strategic mindset, skills, and project ideas to begin your journey as a real AI engineer.

Now it's time to put everything into action — and we've created the tools to help you do exactly that.

Download your exclusive AI BONUSES, including:

- **AI Starter Project Pack** - four GitHub repositories ready to clone, customize, and showcase
- **AI Career Kit** - portfolio templates, resume frameworks, and prompt examples for interviews

These resources complete your training and help turn your learning into tangible results.

SCAN THE QR CODE BELOW TO DOWNLOAD BOTH BONUSES INSTANTLY.

References List

Chapter 1 - AI Engineering Jumpstart: Unlocking the Future

Hornberger, M., Bewersdorff, A., & Nerdel, C. (2023, January 1). *What do university students know about Artificial Intelligence? Development and validation of an AI literacy test.* Computers and Education: Artificial Intelligence. https://doi.org/10.1016/j.caeai.2023.100165

John Hopkins University. (2024, June 14). *The Impact of AI on the Engineering Field.* Johns Hopkins Engineering Online. https://ep.jhu.edu/news/the-impact-of-ai-on-the-engineering-field/

Jankowski, J. (2018, June 1). *The true history of spaced repetition.* SuperMemo. https://www.supermemo.com/en/blog/the-true-history-of-spaced-repetition

Job, A. (2025, June 5). *redShift Recruiting.* RedShift Recruiting. https://www.redshiftrecruiting.com/career-blog/ai-job-search-tools

Northwest, E. (n.d.). *Using Project-Based Blended Learning to Engage Career and Technical Education Students.* Education Northwest. https://educationnorthwest.org/insights/using-project-based-blended-learning-engage-career-and-technical-education-students

Schools, S. (2025, May 9). *Benefits of Project-Based Learning in Online Education.* Sora Schools. https://soraschools.com/blog/benefits-of-project-based-learning-in-online-education

Stine-Morrow, E. A. L., Payne, B. R., Roberts, B. W., Kramer, A. F., Morrow, D. G., Payne, L., Hill, P. L., Jackson, J. J., Gao, X., Noh, S. R., Janke, M. C., & Parisi, J. M. (2014,

December). *Training versus engagement as paths to cognitive enrichment with aging*. Psychology and Aging. https://doi.org/10.1037/a0038244

University Of San Diego. (2024, February 21). *4 Ways AI Impacts the Job Market & Employment Trends*. University of San Diego Online Degrees; University of San Diego. https://onlinedegrees.sandiego.edu/ai-impact-on-job-market/

Why Age 13-19 is ideal for Learning AI: The Science Behind Teen AI Mastery - LearnWithPride. (2025, May 31). Learnwithpride. https://learnwithpride.co.uk/why-age-13-19-is-ideal-for-learning-ai/

luminousmen. (2022). *Practical Guide to Navigating Tech Job Market: Job Search and Networking*. Blog | Iamluminousmen. https://luminousmen.com/post/practical-guide-to-navigating-tech-job-market/

Chapter 2 - AI Engineering Unpacked: The Essentials and the Pitfalls

Artificial Intelligence vs. Machine Learning | CMU. (n.d.). Www.calmu.edu. https://www.calmu.edu/news/artificial-intelligence-vs-machine-learning

Benigni, A. (2025, February 26). *The Future of Software Development in the AI Era*. DEV Community. https://dev.to/alessandro_benigni/the-future-of-software-development-in-the-ai-era-nn2

Chiu, T. K. F., Ahmad, Z., Ismailov, M., & Sanusi, I. T. (2024, June 1). *What are artificial intelligence literacy and competency? A comprehensive framework to support them*. Computers and Education Open. https://doi.org/10.1016/j.caeo.2024.100171

Kalayjian, V. (2024, December 31). *Systems Thinking - Vazken Kalayjian - Medium*. Medium. https://kalayjian.medium.com/systems-thinking-31f25db98433

Masood, A. (2025, May 24). *AI in Project Management — How Generative and Agentic AI Are Redefining Strategy, Execution, and Value Delivery*. Medium. https://medium.com/@adnanmasood/ai-in-project-management-how-generative-and-agentic-ai-are-redefining-strategy-execution-and-ccfd45229e7b

OECD. (2025). *Skill needs and policies in the age of artificial intelligence*. OECD. https://www.oecd.org/en/publications/oecd-employment-outlook-2023_08785bba-en/full-report/skill-needs-and-policies-in-the-age-of-artificial-intelligence_fe530fbf.html

Sharps, S. (2024, November 8). *The Impact of AI on the Labour Market*. Institute.global; Tony Blair Institute. https://institute.global/insights/economic-prosperity/the-impact-of-ai-on-the-labour-market

What Is the AI Development Lifecycle? (2015). Palo Alto Networks. https://www.paloaltonetworks.com/cyberpedia/ai-development-lifecycle

aijobs.net will become foo🦍 - visit foorilla.com! (2024). Aijobs.net. https://aijobs.net/insights/ai-scientist-vs-machine-learning-research-engineer/

de Saint Laurent, C. (2018, November 30). *In defence of machine learning: Debunking the myths of artificial intelligence*. Europe's Journal of Psychology. https://doi.org/10.5964/ejop.v14i4.1823

Chapter 3 - The Tools of an AI Engineer: Your Modern Stack

Breaking Down the Web Application Deployment Process. (n.d.). Western Governors University. https://www.wgu.edu/blog/breaking-down-web-application-deployment-process2311.html

Daily Papers - Hugging Face. (2025). Huggingface.co. https://huggingface.co/papers?q=fine-tuning-as-a-service

Daily Papers - Hugging Face. (2025). Huggingface.co. https://huggingface.co/papers?q=dissemination%20of%20finetuned%20models

MLflow: A Tool for Managing the Machine Learning Lifecycle | MLflow. (2025). Mlflow.org. https://mlflow.org/docs/latest/ml/

MLflow. (2025). Mlflow.org. http://mlflow.org/classical-ml/experiment-tracking

Practical Guide for Model Selection for Real-World Use Cases | OpenAI Cookbook. (2025). Openai.com. https://cookbook.openai.com/examples/partners/model_selection_guide/model_selection_guide

Raman Bazhanau. (2024, October 7). *Preparing FastAPI for Production: A Comprehensive Guide*. Medium. https://medium.com/@ramanbazhanau/preparing-fastapi-for-production-a-comprehensive-guide-d167e693aa2b

Service, D. (2024, April 30). *FastAPI Best Practices: A Condensed Guide with Examples*. DEV Community. https://dev.to/devasservice/fastapi-best-practices-a-condensed-guide-with-examples-3pa5?context=digest

TheTechPencil. (2025, March 17). *OpenAI's New AI Toolkit - TheTechPencil - Medium*. Medium. https://medium.com/@TheTechPencil/openais-new-ai-toolkit-e5e563e26963

Vidya Ugare. (2024). *DOCKER CONTAINERS: REVOLUTIONIZING SOFTWARE DEPLOYMENT AND INFRASTRUCTURE MANAGEMENT*. Madhya Bharti - Humanities and Social Sciences UGC Care Group I Journal (मध्य भारती) ISSN: 0974-0066. https://www.academia.edu/122500019/DOCKER_CONTAINERS_REVOLUTIONIZING_SOFTWARE_DEPLOYMENT_AND_INFRASTRUCTURE_MANAGEMENT

Chapter 4 - Chatbot Wizardry: Building Your First AI Project with OpenAI

Amore Rossouw, & Smuts, H. (2023, January 1). *Key Principles Pertinent to User Experience Design for Conversational User Interfaces: A Conceptual Learning Model*. Lecture Notes in Computer Science. https://doi.org/10.1007/978-3-031-40113-8_17
Building an AI Chatbot Using Python and NLP. (2024, December 6). Alltius.ai; Alltius. https://www.alltius.ai/glossary/complete-guide-to-build-your-ai-chatbot-with-nlp-in-python

Building a Conversational Chatbot with GPT-4: Step-by-Step Guide. (2024). Artiba.org. https://www.artiba.org/blog/building-a-conversational-chatbot-with-gpt-4-step-by-step-guide

Botable Blog | Boost Efficiency: Chatbots & Continuous Feedback Loops in Your QMS. (2025). Botable.ai. https://www.botable.ai/blog/quality-improvement-feedback-loops-using-chatbots

GeeksforGeeks. (2024, January 6). *Develop an LLM Application using Openai*. GeeksforGeeks. https://www.geeksforgeeks.org/develop-an-llm-application-using-openai/

How to Contribute to Open-Source Projects – A Handbook for Beginners. (2023, September 6). FreeCodeCamp.org. https://www.freecodecamp.org/news/how-to-contribute-to-open-source-handbook/

Interactive Programs. (2020). Software Design. https://softdes.olin.edu/docs/projects/interactivity/

Janssen, A., Rodríguez Cardona, D., Passlick, J., & Breitner, M. H. (2022, December). *How to Make chatbots productive – A user-oriented implementation framework*. International Journal of Human-Computer Studies. https://doi.org/10.1016/j.ijhcs.2022.102921

SmythOS - A Comprehensive Guide to Conversational Agents and Chatbot Testing. (2024, November 4). SmythOS. https://smythos.com/ai-agents/conversational-agents/conversational-agents-and-chatbot-testing/

pygpt-net. (2023, April 14). PyPI. https://pypi.org/project/pygpt-net/0.9.3/

Chapter 5 - Going Deeper : Fine-Tuning AI with HuggingFace

AI Fine Tuned Models Strategy. (2025, May). Stratechi.com. https://www.stratechi.com/ai-fine-tuned-models-strategy/

Bhat, A., Coursey, A., Hu, G., Li, S., Nahar, N., Zhou, S., Kästner, C., & Guo, J. L. C. (2023, April 19). *Aspirations and Practice of Model Documentation: Moving the Needle with Nudging and Traceability*. ArXiv.org. https://doi.org/10.1145/3544548.3581518

GeeksforGeeks. (2017, November 21). *Cross Validation in Machine Learning*. GeeksforGeeks. https://www.geeksforgeeks.org/machine-learning/cross-validation-machine-learning/

Kerner, S. M. (2025, June 27). *Why your enterprise AI strategy needs both open and closed models: The TCO reality check*. VentureBeat. https://venturebeat.com/ai/why-your-enterprise-ai-strategy-needs-both-open-and-closed-models-the-tco-reality-check/

Resources for using Hugging Face with Amazon SageMaker AI - Amazon SageMaker AI. (2025). Amazon.com. https://docs.aws.amazon.com/sagemaker/latest/dg/hugging-face.html

Rao, S. (2025, June 14). *The Comprehensive Guide to Fine-tuning LLM - Data Science Collective - Medium*. Medium; Data Science Collective. https://medium.com/data-science-collective/comprehensive-guide-to-fine-tuning-llm-4a8fd4d0e0af

Srivastava, T. (2019, August 6). *Evaluation Metrics Machine Learning*. Analytics Vidhya. https://www.analyticsvidhya.com/blog/2019/08/11-important-model-evaluation-error-metrics/

Schmid, P. (2020). *philschmid-de-blog*. Huggingface.co. https://huggingface.co/datasets/philschmid/philschmid-de-blog

huggingface. (2020). *notebooks/transformers_doc/en/training.ipynb at main · huggingface/notebooks*. GitHub. https://github.com/huggingface/notebooks/blob/main/transformers_doc/en/training.ipynb

Chapter 6 - From Notebook to Web App: Deploying AI with FastAPI and Docker

10 Software Engineering Skills Needed to Lead in the AI Economy - The Quantic Blog. (2025, January 28). Quantic School of Business and Technology.

https://quantic.edu/blog/2025/01/28/10-software-engineering-skills-needed-to-lead-in-the-ai-economy/

AI: Community of Practice | Emerging Technologies. (2022). Columbia.edu. https://etc.cuit.columbia.edu/AI-community-of-practice

API Keys Security & Secrets Management Best Practices - GitGuardian Blog. (2023, March 9). GitGuardian Blog - Code Security for the DevOps Generation. https://blog.gitguardian.com/secrets-api-management/

API Key Best Practices: Keeping Your Keys Safe and Secure | Anthropic Help Center. (2025). Anthropic.com. https://support.anthropic.com/en/articles/9767949-api-key-best-practices-keeping-your-keys-safe-and-secure

Baker, J. (2023, September 21). *Docker Containerization Simplified*. DevOps Pros. https://opspros.com/docker-containerization-simplified/

FastAPI. (2023). *FastAPI*. Fastapi.tiangolo.com. https://fastapi.tiangolo.com/

First Steps - FastAPI. (n.d.). Fastapi.tiangolo.com. https://fastapi.tiangolo.com/tutorial/first-steps/

GeeksforGeeks. (2019, September 17). *Containerization using Docker*. GeeksforGeeks. https://www.geeksforgeeks.org/blogs/containerization-using-docker/

Salerno, P. (2024, November 15). *The Impact of AI and Automation on Software Development: A Deep Dive*. IEEE Chicago Section. https://ieeechicago.org/the-impact-of-ai-and-automation-on-software-development-a-deep-dive/

https://www.srainternational.org/people/srai-jra2. (2025, May 22). *Advancing Research Administration with AI: A Case Study from Emory University*. Srainternational.org. https://www.srainternational.org/blogs/srai-jra2/2025/05/22/advancing-research-administration-with-ai-emory

Chapter 7 - Smart Monitoring: Tracking, Logging, and Improving with MLflow

Adelakun, B. (2022, December 30). *The Impact Of AI On Internal Auditing: Transforming Practices And Ensuring Compliance*. Finance & Accounting Research Journal; Fair East Publishers. https://doi.org/10.51594/farj.v4i6.1316

Anglen, J. (2024, September 19). *AI Agent Predictive Device Failure Detector: A Comprehensive Guide*. Rapidinnovation.io; Rapid Innovation. https://www.rapidinnovation.io/post/ai-agent-predictive-device-failure-detector

Crudu, A. (2024, March 22). *Leveraging Machine Learning for Predictive Testing in Software Development - Boost Quality and Efficiency*. Moldstud.com; MoldStud - Custom Software Development Company. https://moldstud.com/articles/p-leveraging-machine-learning-for-predictive-testing-in-software-development

How to add MLflow to your Kedro workflow — kedro 0.19.14 documentation. (2025, March 10). Kedro.org. https://docs.kedro.org/en/stable/integrations/mlflow.html

MLflow Dataset Tracking | MLflow. (2024). Mlflow.org. https://mlflow.org/docs/latest/ml/dataset/

M. Harshvardhan, Curtland, C., Hwang, J., VanDam, C., Ghozeil, A., Neto, P. A., Marie, F., & Liu, C. (2025, May 29). *Print Demand Forecasting with Machine Learning at HP Inc*. INFORMS Journal on Applied Analytics; Institute for Operations Research and the Management Sciences. https://doi.org/10.1287/inte.2024.0126

MLflow with Optuna: Hyperparameter Optimization and Tracking | MLflow. (2023). Mlflow.org. https://mlflow.org/docs/latest/ml/traditional-ml/tutorials/hyperparameter-tuning/notebooks/hyperparameter-tuning-with-child-runs

Oyefolu, O. (2025, January 14). *Introduction to MLflow: Tracking, Models, and Projects*. Medium. https://medium.com/@laoluoyefolu/introduction-to-mlflow-tracking-models-and-projects-a84c4cac2335

Slashdot. (2025). Slashdot.org. https://slashdot.org/software/ml-experiment-tracking/

Software Engineering Just Got Smarter: Inside the Rise of AI-Native Delivery. (2025). Ideas2it.com. https://www.ideas2it.com/blogs/ai-in-software-engineering

Chapter 8 - From Projects to Paychecks: Using Your Work to Land AI Jobs

Brown, F. (2017, February 14). *TechnologyAdvice Guide to Applicant Tracking Systems*. TechnologyAdvice; TechnologyAdvice. https://technologyadvice.com/applicant-tracking-systems/

Best Practices for Optimizing a GitHub Profile? · community · Discussion #154875. (2025, March 24). GitHub. https://github.com/orgs/community/discussions/154875

Dwivedi, Y. K. (2023, August). *"So What If ChatGPT Wrote it?" Multidisciplinary Perspectives on opportunities, Challenges and Implications of Generative Conversational AI for research, Practice and Policy*. International Journal of Information Management. https://doi.org/10.1016/j.ijinfomgt.2023.102642

Fauvel, W. (2025). *AI-driven skill shift: The need for continuous upskilling. AMPLYFI.* Retrieved from https://amplyfi.com/blog/ai-driven-skill-shift-the-need-for-continuous-upskilling/

Free Resume Tools Archives · Page 2 of 7 · ResuFit. (2025, April 5). ResuFit. https://www.resufit.com/blog/tag/free-resume-tools/page/2/

How to Optimize a LinkedIn Profile in 2024? (2024, May 22). WORK on PEAK. https://workonpeak.org/how-to-optimize-a-linkedin-profile-in-2024/

Hall, B. (2024, April 12). *101 real-world gen AI use cases from the world's leading organizations*. Google Cloud Blog. https://cloud.google.com/transform/101-real-world-generative-ai-use-cases-from-industry-leaders

Loh, H.-H., Beauchene, V., Lukic, V., & Shenoy, R. (2024, October 8). *Five Must-Haves for Effective AI Upskilling*. BCG Global. https://www.bcg.com/publications/2024/five-must-haves-for-ai-upskilling

Resumes, Cover Letters, and LinkedIn - Making Waves Education Foundation. (2025, April 22). Making Waves Education Foundation. https://making-waves.org/career/resumes-cover-letters-and-linkedin/

Sonu, N. R. (2022, July 18). *How to create an effective GitHub project README?* Masai School. https://www.masaischool.com/blog/how-to-create-an-effective-github-project-readme-2/

About the Author

Nathan J. Halridge is a computer engineer, educator, and mentor with over 20 years of experience in software development and more than a decade of hands-on expertise in the field of artificial intelligence.
After working for some of the leading tech companies in the U.S., he chose to devote himself to teaching, with the goal of making AI accessible to everyone—from transitioning professionals to aspiring young learners.

With an academic background in Engineering and a career built between Silicon Valley and innovative startups, Nathan is known for his clear and practical approach to technical learning.
He has taught at several American universities, contributed to major open-source projects, and trained hundreds of students, guiding them from zero to real-world applications.

Through this book, he shares field-tested tools, strategies, and insights to help every reader build a solid foundation in AI engineering—no shortcuts, just real, actionable guidance.

Your Review Can Make a Difference...

If this book helped you better understand AI engineering or sparked new ideas for your own projects, I would truly appreciate reading your thoughts on Amazon.

Your review is not only a valuable support for this work — it can also help many other readers find a practical and reliable guide on their journey.

Thank you sincerely in advance for sharing your thoughts about this book. And thank you from the bottom of my heart for placing your trust in me and for choosing to read **AI Engineering Starter Kit**.

[Scan the QR code or click here to leave a review]

www.ingramcontent.com/pod-product-compliance
Lightning Source LLC
Chambersburg PA
CBHW061355240926
51846CB00007B/1412